G000155445

Building Mobile Applications Using Kendo UI Mobile and ASP.NET Web API

Get started with Kendo UI Mobile and learn how to integrate it with HTTP-based services built using ASP.NET Web API

Nishanth Nair

Ragini Kumbhat Bhandari

PUBLISHING

BIRMINGHAM - MUMBAI

Building Mobile Applications Using Kendo UI Mobile and ASP.NET Web API

First published: September 2013

Production Reference: 1060913

Published by Packt Publishing Ltd.
Livery Place
35 Livery Street
Birmingham B3 2PB, UK.

ISBN 978-1-78216-092-2

www.packtpub.com

Cover Image by Nishanth Nair (Nair.nishanth@gmail.com)

Credits

Authors
Nishanth Nair
Ragini Kumbhat Bhandari

Reviewers
David J McClelland
Morteza Sahragard
Brian Seekford

Acquisition Editor
Martin Bell

Lead Technical Editor
Sweny M. Sukumaran

Technical Editors
Akashdeep Kundu
Shiny Poojary

Project Coordinator
Arshad Sopariwala
Priyanka Goel

Proofreader
Joanna McMahon

Indexer
Hemangini Bari

Graphics
Abhinash Sahu

Production Coordinator
Pooja Chiplunkar

Cover Work
Pooja Chiplunkar

About the Authors

Nishanth Nair is a Mobile Solutions Architect, currently working as a Consultant for Sears Holdings Corporation. He holds a bachelor's degree in Computer Science and Engineering and has extensive experience with .NET technologies working for companies such as Accenture, McAfee, and Neudesic. He is a Microsoft Certified Application Developer and a Microsoft Certified Technology Specialist. In his free time, he likes to play cricket, tennis, and watch movies.

Acknowledgments

I would like to thank my wife Soumia, for all her support and patience while I wrote the book. Thank you for being such a wonderful wife! Many thanks to my parents, Sreedevi and Ramachandran Nair, and to my sister Nishi Nair for their love and encouragement.

Thanks to my friends Santhosh Karuthethil, Krishnanunni Pattiyil, Ashin Das, Aneesh Pulukkul, Sinto Antony, Anish Vasudevan, Mahesh Nair, and Lakshmi Ravi for being great friends forever. Also I would like to thank my ex-colleagues and buddies at Davita VillageHealth, Anita Nair, Alison Massey, Patrick D'Coster, Satheesh Ambat, Srinivasa Rao, Aruna Shanthaveerappa, and Sarika Goel for all their support and encouragement.

Thanks to my buddy and mentor Rajiv Kolagani who is always an inspiration to me.

Thanks to all my NECAB Core friends, Balachandran Warrier, Sudeesh Yezhuvath, Prakash Bare, Sahasranam, Promod PP, Snehaprabha, Rajeev G, Aji John, Jojy Varghese, Manoj KC, Sivaram P, Kiran, Syam Chand, Hitha, Dhanya V, Minu P, Ragesh, and all the others for being best friends forever!

Many thanks to the Packt Publishing team who made this book happen – especially Martin Bell, Sweny Sukumaran, Priyanka Goel, Arshad Sopariwala, Shiny Poojary, and Akashdeep Kundu.

I am greatly indebted to the reviewers of this book, Brian Seekford, David McClelland and Morteza Sahragard for the wonderful job they have done.

Ragini Kumbhat Bhandari is working at eMids Technologies Private Limited as a Technical Lead. She holds a Master of Computer Applications degree in Computer Science and she is a Microsoft Certified Technology Specialist.

During the course of her career she has worked extensively on .NET and mobile technologies. She finds happiness in sharing knowledge and educating the next generation of software professionals. Apart from spending time on the computer, she likes listening to music.

I would like to thank my parents, D.S. Kumbhat and Sheela Kumbhat, for their encouragement, patience, and support. I would like to thank my company eMids for providing a work culture which inspired me to contribute beyond work. Many thanks to the Packt Publishing team and the reviewers of the book.

About the Reviewers

David J McClelland has been creating cutting-edge software and content that bridges design, development, and information for over 20 years. He is currently a Principal User Interface Engineer, developing software to manage distributed devices via the Cloud.

> I would like to thank my family for encouraging many of my technical and artistic interests.

Morteza Sahragard was born in Iran, and received his Bachelor of Science degree in Software Engineering. He started programming in the middle of 2000 with Pascal and then C++. With the increasing popularity of the .NET platform, he turned to the Microsoft programming framework and since then he has been involved in various kinds of applications, from Windows to Web, Network to Multimedia, Mobile to highly distributed systems, and so on. In the middle of 2006 he created www.30sharp.com, which is nowadays a famous and well-known tutorial website about technical programming and designing stuff (in Persian). At the moment, he is working as a Senior .NET Developer in an international IT company in Armenia. You can also find him at his English blog: http://weblogs.asp.net/morteza.

Brian Seekford is an experienced software engineer and architect, and is the CEO of Seekford Solutions, Inc. He works with client-side, server-side, and mobile technologies with an emphasis on large scale n-tier systems. The primary technologies he utilizes are the .NET platform for the client and server side, and JavaScript/HTML5 for mobile development. He has worked for Walt Disney World, BP, GM, Delta, PwC, and others who utilize a variety of technologies and hardware. He also built and sold ActiveX controls for network communications and web technologies for 11 years.

I would like to thank my wife and children for putting up with me.

www.PacktPub.com

Support files, eBooks, discount offers, and more

You might want to visit www.PacktPub.com for support files and downloads related to your book.

Did you know that Packt offers eBook versions of every book published, with PDF and ePub files available? You can upgrade to the eBook version at www.PacktPub.com and as a print book customer, you are entitled to a discount on the eBook copy. Get in touch with us at service@packtpub.com for more details.

At www.PacktPub.com, you can also read a collection of free technical articles, sign up for a range of free newsletters and receive exclusive discounts and offers on Packt books and eBooks.

http://PacktLib.PacktPub.com

Do you need instant solutions to your IT questions? PacktLib is Packt's online digital book library. Here, you can access, read and search across Packt's entire library of books.

Why Subscribe?

- Fully searchable across every book published by Packt
- Copy and paste, print and bookmark content
- On demand and accessible via web browser

Free Access for Packt account holders

If you have an account with Packt at www.PacktPub.com, you can use this to access PacktLib today and view nine entirely free books. Simply use your login credentials for immediate access.

Table of Contents

Preface

The sudden explosion of mobile devices has made mobile apps development one of the hottest career fields for programmers. The global smartphone/tablet market shared by multiple platforms posed a serious question to mobile application developers and companies, as every mobile platform has different development frameworks and programming languages to develop native applications.

How can we achieve **WORA (Write Once, Run Anywhere)**?

The obvious solution was HTML5, which is supported by all the latest browsers and has great support for developing rich user interfaces. With the introduction of platforms such as PhoneGap, which exposes the native OS APIs to apps developed in HTML5/JavaScript and CSS3, HTML5-based applications became a double-edged sword. They can be developed using one code base and deployed as a mobile website as well as mobile apps which can be installed on different platforms, as opposed to developing native apps which will result in multiple code bases if multiple platforms are targeted. The availability of a large number of web developers in the industry who understand HTML, JavaScript, and CSS added a boost to the shifting direction of mobile apps development towards HTML5. As the demand increased for more and more mobile applications, both in enterprise and consumer areas, different types of HTML5-based development frameworks surfaced and are still surfacing!

Kendo UI Mobile from Telerik is one of the fastest growing HTML5- and jQuery-based cross-browser mobile applications development frameworks. Kendo UI Mobile distinguishes itself from other frameworks by providing adaptive native UI rendering out of the box, without any extra coding, and supporting the Kendo base application development framework. While other mobile development frameworks concentrate on the UI part only, Kendo UI provides support for end-to-end, client-side development.

As the world is getting closer to the HTTP protocol, Web APIs (services which are exposed over plain HTTP) are gaining momentum. ASP.NET Web API helps to build powerful Web APIs, which can be consumed by a rich set of clients and is now the number one choice for .NET developers to build RESTful applications.

This book will introduce you to Kendo UI Mobile and will show you how to build an end-to-end mobile app using ASP.NET Web API as the service backend.

What this book covers

Chapter 1, Building a Mobile Application Using HTML5, helps a programmer, who is relatively new to the mobile applications development world, pick up on this journey to build an end-to-end app using Kendo UI Mobile. The chapter details different types of mobile applications such as native, hybrid and mobile websites, an introduction to Kendo UI Mobile, and wraps up with mobile applications design guidelines.

Chapter 2, Building Your First Mobile Application, introduces you to Kendo UI Mobile code in detail, and some screens for the Movie Tickets app will be developed explaining views, layouts, navigation, and more. From this chapter we get our hands dirty and write some really cool code.

Chapter 3, Service Layer with ASP.NET Web API, introduces you to one of the latest additions to Microsoft .NET stack, ASP.NET Web API. We will see routing, parameter binding, content negotiation, token-based authentication, authorization, and write some API methods which will be used for the sample Movie Tickets application. Readers not from the Microsoft background can skip this chapter as well as writing your own services with the same functionality on a platform of your choice or use the service hosted by us on the Internet. The frontend Kendo UI Mobile client application is independent of the backend API technology and will work with any service platform as long as it accepts and returns the same JSON data.

Chapter 4, Integration Using Framework Elements, discusses the common Kendo Framework elements such as DataSource, Templates, and MVVM, which are used in both mobile and web application development. Then we will start backend integration with the Movie Tickets app by building the User Account screen, discussing the Revealing Module Pattern and the application architecture.

Chapter 5, Exploring Mobile Widgets, introduces you to the core of the Kendo UI Mobile Framework, the Mobile widgets. We will dive deep into widgets such as ListView, Button, ButtonGroup, and so on. Using the provided jsFiddle examples, users can play around with the sample code.

Chapter 6, ActionSheet, ModalView, and More Widgets, continues on from the previous chapter, and we will explore more Kendo UI Mobile widgets hands-on.

Chapter 7, Movie Tickets Application – Complete Integration, completes our Movie Tickets sample application by integrating with Kendo UI Mobile widgets, framework elements, and the ASP.NET Web API service.

Who this book is for

This book is intended for novice and expert programmers with a web development background who want to build mobile applications or mobile websites for enterprise as well as consumer domains. A basic understanding of HTML, CSS, and jQuery is required to make good use of this book.

What you need for this book

The following software are required to make full use of this book:

- **Kendo UI Mobile**: Free trial or commercial licensed version ($199 per developer)
- **jQuery 1.8.1**: Free
- **Ripple Emulator**: Free
- **MS Visual Studio 2010/2012 Express edition, ASP.NET MVC4**: These are available as free downloads and are required only if you are a .NET programmer and are interested in exploring ASP.NET Web API.

Conventions

In this book, you will find a number of styles of text that distinguish between different kinds of information. Here are some examples of these styles, and an explanation of their meaning.

Code words in text, database table names, folder names, filenames, file extensions, pathnames, dummy URLs, user input, and Twitter handles are shown as follows: "Now let's create an action method in `MoviesController.cs`, which calls the `GetMovieList` BLL method."

A block of code is set as follows:

```
public class TrailerBO
{
    public string MovieName { get; set; }
    public string VideoUrl { get; set; }
}
```

When we wish to draw your attention to a particular part of a code block, the relevant lines or items are set in bold:

```
<!-- Movies main view --->
<div data-role="view" id="mt-home-main-view" data-title="Movies"
        data-init="MovieTickets.movieList.initialize"
        data-model="MovieTickets.movieList.viewModel"
        data-layout="mt-main-layout" class="no-backbutton">
```

Any command-line input or output is written as follows:

customEvent fired

customEvent fired with data: Kendo UI is cool!

New terms and **important words** are shown in bold. Words that you see on the screen, in menus or dialog boxes for example, appear in the text like this: Two buttons, **Open Left** and **Open Right**, are placed on the NavBar widget in the layout of the views, which can be clicked to open the Drawer widgets as shown in the following code:

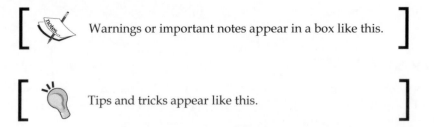

Warnings or important notes appear in a box like this.

Tips and tricks appear like this.

Reader feedback

Feedback from our readers is always welcome. Let us know what you think about this book—what you liked or may have disliked. Reader feedback is important for us to develop titles that you really get the most out of.

To send us general feedback, simply send an e-mail to feedback@packtpub.com, and mention the book title via the subject of your message.

If there is a topic that you have expertise in and you are interested in either writing or contributing to a book, see our author guide on www.packtpub.com/authors.

Customer support

Now that you are the proud owner of a Packt book, we have a number of things to help you to get the most from your purchase.

Downloading the example code and graphics

You can download the example code files for all Packt books you have purchased from your account at http://www.packtpub.com. If you purchased this book elsewhere, you can visit http://www.packtpub.com/support and register to have the files e-mailed directly to you.

You can download the colored graphics from: http://www.packtpub.com/sites/default/files/downloads/0922OT_ColoredImages.pdf

Errata

Although we have taken every care to ensure the accuracy of our content, mistakes do happen. If you find a mistake in one of our books—maybe a mistake in the text or the code—we would be grateful if you would report this to us. By doing so, you can save other readers from frustration and help us improve subsequent versions of this book. If you find any errata, please report them by visiting http://www.packtpub.com/submit-errata, selecting your book, clicking on the **errata submission form** link, and entering the details of your errata. Once your errata are verified, your submission will be accepted and the errata will be uploaded on our website, or added to any list of existing errata, under the Errata section of that title. Any existing errata can be viewed by selecting your title from http://www.packtpub.com/support.

Piracy

Piracy of copyright material on the Internet is an ongoing problem across all media. At Packt, we take the protection of our copyright and licenses very seriously. If you come across any illegal copies of our works, in any form, on the Internet, please provide us with the location address or website name immediately so that we can pursue a remedy.

Please contact us at copyright@packtpub.com with a link to the suspected pirated material.

We appreciate your help in protecting our authors, and our ability to bring you valuable content.

Questions

You can contact us at questions@packtpub.com if you are having a problem with any aspect of the book, and we will do our best to address it.

1
Building a Mobile Application Using HTML5

The world is going mobile and millions of smart phones are activated daily. As a result, more and more mobile applications are developed for consumers, and enterprise software products are also slowly but steadily joining the revolution. More and more businesses are convinced that in order to sustain, they need to be in the mobile space. You are a web developer and one fine morning your manager tells you, "We now need to focus on the mobile platforms. Get ready!" or you want to develop a mobile app which needs to be deployed to one or more mobile app stores. There are many factors that play a part in choosing the appropriate mobile development platform, such as your development skills, native functionalities, security, offline capability, and support for multiple platforms. In this chapter, we will see different approaches for developing mobile applications and understand why HTML5 is a popular choice for cross-platform development. Then we will have an introduction to Kendo UI Mobile and will go over some design principles for mobile applications.

In this chapter we will cover:

- Native versus hybrid versus mobile websites
- HTML5 and CSS3
- Kendo UI – building cross-browser apps made easy
- Kendo UI Mobile
- HTML5 mobile web application design guidelines

Native versus hybrid versus mobile websites

As you may already be aware, there are three ways to develop a mobile device compatible application: native, hybrid, or mobile website.

Native apps are coded in a programming language specific to a platform, namely, Objective C for iOS, Java for Android, and so on. Native applications run faster, have access to all device APIs and features, and provide a better user experience. Since native apps are built for a particular platform, the entire application needs to be rewritten if a native application needs to run on another platform. This will create code duplication, maintenance headache, budget increase, and the need to have multiple development teams (specializing in a certain platform) working on the same business rules. Typically, games and applications which require high performance are developed as pure native apps.

Hybrid apps are written using pure web technologies (such as CSS, HTML, and JavaScript) and they run on the device in a native container using the device's browser engine. Hybrid apps are usually packaged using tools such as PhoneGap, which helps the app to access device-specific APIs and hardware features. WebKit rendering engine is used in platforms such as iOS, Android, and Blackberry to render the web-based script/code to be displayed in a web view control of the native platform. Since Hybrid apps are created using a native app shell, they can be distributed using app stores too. Icenium by Telerik is a cloud-based, all-in-one development environment to package, test, and deploy hybrid applications. PhoneGap is another commonly used tool for packaging web apps for deployment on multiple mobile platforms.

Mobile websites are accessed using a URL and run in the mobile device's browser. They can be developed using server-side technologies, such as ASP.NET and PHP, and can be deployed and updated without any approval process from an app store. If the mobile website is written using pure web technologies (HTML, CSS, and JavaScript) or using frameworks based on them, such as jQuery, Kendo UI, and jQuery Mobile, mobile websites can be packaged to be installed as a hybrid application without much effort. A major drawback of mobile websites is that only device features that are exposed through the browser can be accessed, and this makes a mobile website suitable for content-based applications. There is no single solution which is suitable for all the scenarios. Selection of a methodology will depend on a number of factors, such as the skill sets you have, budget, time lines, and update frequency.

Kendo UI Mobile is an ideal platform for developing hybrid apps and mobile websites. During the course of this book, we will create a Movie Tickets application using Kendo UI Mobile which will be treated as a mobile website initially and then, towards the end of the book, it will be packaged using PhoneGap as a mobile app and deployed to Android as well as the iOS devices.

HTML5 and CSS3

HTML5, jQuery, and CSS3 are the new mantra for developing cutting-edge web applications. When we say web, it includes the standard websites/applications, mobile websites/applications, as well as hybrid applications. Even though this book is about Kendo UI Mobile, it's important to have an idea about the underlying technologies behind the Kendo UI Mobile framework, namely, HTML5, CSS3, and jQuery. Let's take a high-level view at HTML5 and CSS3 technologies briefly before we take a deep dive into Kendo UI Mobile. Since we expect the readers of this book to have knowledge in jQuery, we won't be discussing the basics of jQuery here.

HTML5 – Steve Jobs made me famous

HTML5 shot to fame among the Internet public when Steve Jobs famously announced the death of Flash on the iOS devices and endorsed HTML5 as the future, as it helps to build advanced graphics, typography, animations, and transitions without relying on third-party browser plugins.

HTML5 is a markup language specification that is comprised of a significant number of features, technologies, and APIs that allow content developers to create a rich and interactive experience. HTML5 is still in the recommendation stage, but many browsers already implement a significant portion of the specification. This poses a challenge for developers as they need to figure out which browsers support which features before kick starting an HTML5 project.

Main features of HTML5

Even though the specification for HTML5 is not complete yet, tons of features are already implemented by mainstream browsers. The following are some of the main features of HTML5 as it stands as of today:

• Application cache to support offline web apps	• Geolocation	• Server-sent events
• Audio and video	• Indexed DB	• WebSocket API
• Canvas API	• MathML	• Web storage
• Cross-document messaging	• Microdata	• Web Workers
• Drag-and-drop	• **Scalable Vector Graphics (SVG)**	• XMLHttpRequest Level 2

 `http://html5rocks.com` from Google is a very good website for HTML5 reference with tons of tutorials, articles, and other resources.

Who is behind the HTML5 specification?

There are three different organizations behind the development of the HTML5 specification: **W3C (World Wide Web Consortium)**, **WHATWG (Web Hypertext Application Technology Working Group)**, and **IETF (Internet Engineering Task Force)**. As a result, there are two versions of the HTML5 specification maintained by W3C and WHATWG, which can be found at `http://www.w3.org/TR/html5/` and `http://whatwg.org/html` respectively. IETF comprises of the groups responsible for Internet protocols such as HTTP, and handles the WebSocket protocol which is used by the WebSocket API of HTML5.

Two different versions of HTML5 is not a matter of concern as the WHATWG version is considered as a living standard (meaning there will be constant development and versions no longer will be applied) and W3C is planning to create a single definitive standard, which WHATWG calls a snapshot of their living standard.

The WHATWG effort is focused on developing the canonical description of HTML and related technologies (meaning fixing bugs, adding new features, and generally tracking implementations), while W3C will continue the HTML5 specification work, focusing on a single definitive standard.

A sample HTML5 page

Now let's get our hands dirty and take a look at a simple HTML5 page:

```
<!DOCTYPE HTML>
<html>
  <head>
    <meta charset="utf-8">
    <title>Our first HTML5 page </title>
  </head>
  <body>
    <header>
      <h1>Sample HTML5 Structure</h1>
      <nav>
        <ul>
          <li><a href="#">Link1</a></li>
          <li><a href="#">Link2</a></li>
        </ul>
      </nav>
    </header>
    <section>
      <h1>Main Section</h1>
      <h2>This is a sample HTML5 Page</h2>
      <article>
        <p>Article 1 goes here</p>
      </article>
      <article>
        <p>Article 2 goes here</p>
      </article>
    </section>
    <footer>
      <p>Footer goes here</p>
    </footer>
  </body>
</html>
```

Downloading the example code

You can download the example code files for all Packt books you have purchased from your account at http://www.packtpub.com. If you purchased this book elsewhere, you can visit http://www.packtpub.com/support and register to have the files e-mailed directly to you.

DOCTYPE and character encodings

The DOCTYPE declaration for HTML5 is very simple: `<!DOCTYPE HTML>`

This line needs to be added at the top of every HTML5 page that we create. The new DOCTYPE declaration is plain and simple, unlike the lengthy and hard to remember ones in HTML4 shown as follows:

```
<!DOCTYPE HTML PUBLIC "-//W3C//DTD HTML 4.01//EN"
"http://www.w3.org/TR/html4/strict.dtd">
<!DOCTYPE HTML PUBLIC "-//W3C//DTD HTML 4.01 Frameset//EN"
"http://www.w3.org/TR/html4/frameset.dtd">
```

All the latest browsers will look at the new DOCTYPE declaration and switch the contents into standard mode.

Like the DOCTYPE declaration, the character set declaration is also simplified in HTML5 as shown as follows:

```
<meta charset="UTF-8">
```

The `meta charset` attribute in a meta element is used instead of a pragma directive as in HTML4.

This is how a typical character encoding looks in HTML4:

```
<meta http-equiv="Content-type" content="text/html;charset=UTF-8">
```

Some new HTML5 tags

As highlighted in the earlier code, you can see some new HTML5 tags which are semantic markups. Semantic markups describe their meaning or purpose clearly to the browser and to the developer. In HTML4, we used the `<div>` tag to define a division in a page, but it never provided any details about the contents and had no specific meaning. To make sense, developers used to add an `id` attribute and provide a meaningful ID such as `sectionHeader`, `footer`, and `navLinks` as follows:

```
<div id="sectionHeader"> </div>
```

The semantic elements such as `<header>`, `<footer>`, and `<nav>` were added in to HTML5 as a result of mining billions of web pages, for figuring out what common IDs and CSS class names the developers use most often, and for selecting a small subset to be added in to the HTML5 specification. It made perfect sense as this will help search engines and accessibility tools to crawl the web pages easily and developers can work on neat HTML code.

Let's now checkout some of the new semantic markups we used in our sample HTML5 page.

<header>

The <header> element represents a group of introductory or navigational aids. Typically <header> will be the first element in a page. It is intended to usually contain the section's heading (an h1–h6 element or an hgroup element), but this is not a requirement. The header element can also be used to wrap a section's table of contents, a search form, or any relevant logos.

<nav>

The <nav> element represents a section with navigation links to other pages or to sections inside a page. This element is primarily intended for sections that consist of major navigation blocks. Usually footers will have a short list of links to various pages of a site. The <footer> element alone is sufficient for such cases, while a <nav> element can also be used, but it is usually unnecessary.

The following are some more places where you can think about adding the <nav> element:

- Bread Crumbs
- Table of Contents
- Side Navigation

<section>

The <section> element represents a generic section of a document or application. A section, in this context, is a thematic grouping of the following contents:

- Chapter
- Various tabbed pages in a tabbed dialog box
- Numbered sections of a thesis

A website's home page could be split into sections for an introduction, news items, and contact information. It is a segment of content that you will consider storing as a record in a database.

The <section> element is appropriate only if the contents would be listed explicitly in the document's outline.

\<article\>

The \<article\> element represents an independent section of content such as a blog post, a comment, and a magazine article. An article should be an independent entity and it should be possible to distribute or reuse it even when the surrounding contents are removed.

\<footer\>

The \<footer\> element represents information about the containing element such as links to related content or copyright information. Footers need not be added at the end of the section even though it is the usual practice.

 http://html5test.com/ is a great website to test your browser's HTML5 compatibility.

CSS3

CSS3 is the latest version of CSS, that unlike CSS2 (which is a single large specification of CSS) is divided into multiple modules which are documented and worked upon separately. Work on the CSS3 specification started back in 1998 as soon as the specifications for CSS2 were complete, and it is still undergoing updates.

CSS3 helps in adding life to a web page by animating its elements, applying different effects such as gradients, shadows, multiple backgrounds, and opacity, and much more without using images or client-side code as done with previous versions of CSS. CSS3 helps to improve performance of the application as CSS files are cached on the client side and use hardware acceleration technique for animations on supported browsers.

CSS3 has over 50 modules published from the CSS Working Group such as Media Queries, Namespaces, Color, Animations, Backgrounds and Borders, Selectors, and 2D/3D Transformations.

Let's see using a quick example, how easy it is to apply rounder border, transformation, and shadow to an HTML element using CSS3.

First, let's define a simple `div` element and add some styles to it:

```html
<!DOCTYPE HTML>
<html>
  <head>
    <style type="text/css">
    div#myDiv
    {
      width: 200px;
      height: 100px;
      background-color: #A3D1FF;
      border: 1px solid black;
      margin: 10px;
      padding: 5px;
    }
    </style>
  </head>
  <body>
    <div style="margin: 75px">
      <div id="myDiv">
      I am an HTML div
      </div>
    </div>
  </body>
</html>
```

The HTML is rendered as shown in the following figure:

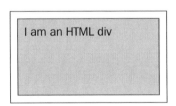

Now, we need to rotate this div by 40 degrees, add rounded corners to the border, and add a shadow to the box. In CSS3, achieving these requirements is very easy using few lines of code. Add the following CSS3 properties to the CSS definition of our HTML document:

```css
border-radius: 10px;
box-shadow: 8px 8px 1px gray;
transform: rotate(40deg);
-ms-transform: rotate(40deg); /* IE 9 */
-webkit-transform: rotate(40deg); /* Safari and Chrome */
```

On reloading the HTML page, we can see our div has transformed to this new look:

Kendo UI – building cross-browser apps made easy

Now that we have had enough of an overview, let's get started with the real thing: **Kendo UI Framework** from Telerik. Telerik has always been in the forefront for providing **Rapid Application Development (RAD)** tools for the developers and Kendo UI Framework is the recent addition to the Telerik RAD stack for building HTML5, jQuery, and CSS3 based cross-browser applications.

The only external dependency to using Kendo UI is jQuery. Developing applications using Kendo UI is straightforward and the setup requires only referencing the jQuery, Kendo JavaScript, and CSS files in your HTML page.

> The word Kendo means "Way of the Sword", which is a traditional Japanese style of fencing.

The Kendo UI Framework can be broadly classified into:

- Kendo UI Widgets
- Kendo UI Framework elements

The Kendo widgets use HTML5, CSS3, and jQuery to build powerful web applications without using multiple third-party frameworks and plugins, as in the case with some of the other HTML5/jQuery frameworks.

Kendo UI widgets are the UI elements that we really "see" once the application is developed such as the buttons, drop-down list, and tree view. The Framework elements are the invisible entities such as DataSource, Templates, and MVVM, which helps in integrating the data with the widgets. For simplicity, if we consider an application built using Kendo UI as a building, the UI widgets are the bricks and the Framework elements are the cement which helps the bricks to stick together.

Kendo UI widgets

Kendo UI widgets can be classified into three groups:

- **Kendo UI Web**: These are used for touch-enabled desktop development
- **Kendo UI DataViz**: These are used for desktop and mobile data visualizations
- **Kendo UI Mobile**: These are used for mobile application development

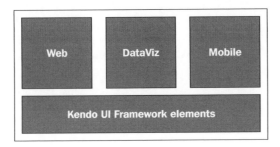

Kendo UI architecture

Even though Kendo UI Web and DataViz are outside the scope of this book, it is a good idea to have an understanding of these two as well, as all the three widget groups inter-operate seamlessly and there is a good chance that in a big project more than one widget group needs to be used.

Kendo UI Web

Kendo UI Web widgets are used for building keyboard/mouse input as well as touch-based traditional cross-browser web applications. As of today, there are 22 widgets available in the Kendo UI Web widgets collection. All Kendo UI Web widgets provide full support for touch-screen devices, such as the iPad, iPhone, and Android, so that the web applications can be accessed on a wide array of devices with varying input options.

Even though the Kendo UI Web framework uses modern HTML5 and CSS3 based widgets, it supports older browsers such as IE7 and IE8 by implementing graceful degradation.

 More information about Kendo UI Web can be found at:
`http://www.kendoui.com/web.aspx`

Kendo UI DataViz

Kendo UI DataViz widgets help to build cutting-edge, touch-aware charts and dashboards using HTML5. Thanks to built-in hardware acceleration, DataViz widgets use less CPU resources and thereby provide maximum performance for all animations and rendering. DataViz graphics are rendered on the client using SVG with a fallback to VML for legacy browsers.

DataViz supports the following charts and gauges widgets:

Chart Types	Gauges Types
Area	Radial
Bar	Linear
Bubble	
Line	
Donut	
Pie	
Scatter	

 And just like the Web widgets, DataViz supports older browsers such as IE7 and IE8 by mixing their limited HTML5 support (if any) and graceful degradation. DataViz fully supports the latest mobile browsers and so it can be used both in desktop web apps as well as in mobile apps. More information about Kendo UI DataViz can be found at: `http://www.kendoui.com/dataviz.aspx`

Kendo UI Mobile

Kendo UI Mobile is the third group of the Kendo UI widget stack that helps to build HTML5-based mobile websites as well as hybrid mobile applications. Kendo UI Mobile features adaptive rendering technique which helps applications' look and feel to adapt to the platform on which it is viewed. Without any configurations or extra code, an application built on Kendo UI Mobile looks like Android on an Android device, iOS on an iOS device, and so on. At the time of writing of this book, Kendo UI Mobile supports iOS, Android, BlackBerry, and Windows 8 platforms.

Now you might have this question: "What if I need a single look and feel across all the devices on which the app is viewed?" Recently, Kendo has released a **Universal Mobile Theme** using which the developers can create a consistent look and feel across different platforms. If you are not using this new theme, a single configuration to force a specific platform while instantiating the mobile app will do the trick! Once we force the UI to render using a particular platform's look and feel and then modifying, the corresponding CSS files for that platform will ensure the same look and feel across multiple platforms.

 Kendo also provides a Mobile Theme Builder to customize the styles of the mobile widgets: http://demos.kendoui.com/mobilethemebuilder/index.html

Server wrappers

If you are a server-side programmer who works on ASP.NET MVC, JSP, or PHP, there is good news for you: Kendo UI has server wrappers available for ASP.NET MVC, PHP, and JSP which automatically generates the necessary HTML and JavaScript to configure, render, and initialize your Kendo UI widgets (Web and Mobile) and charts (DataViz). The server wrappers emits Kendo UI JavaScript and provides full access to the Kendo UI client-side API so that the UI can be manipulated from the client-side too once the web page is rendered.

 You can read more about the server wrappers here: http://www.kendoui.com/server-wrappers.aspx

HTML5 mobile web application design guidelines

Developing applications for mobile devices is quite different from developing websites for desktops and laptops. There are a wide range of mobile devices available with varying screen sizes and processing powers. Mobile devices access the Internet with varying bandwidth; they can be connected to a Wi-Fi network and in an instant they can go to a slow 2G network. All these factors make mobile applications development different from traditional web applications development.

Here are some guidelines which will help developers while building a mobile web application:

- **Animations with CSS3 rather than with jQuery**: Whenever possible use CSS3 animations as they are handled in the browser natively so that it can make use of the hardware resources thus increasing the performance.

- **Responsive design using CSS3 media queries**: Mobile devices these days have varying screen sizes and it's a basic expectation that a mobile web app will fit on the screen of the device requesting the application. Responsive designs using CSS3 media queries help the same code base provide an optimal viewing experience on a wide range of devices.

- **Use CSS3 gradients instead of images**: Using CSS3, we can provide gradients in your web page without using specifically cut images. This helps to preserve bandwidth by not having images travelling over the wire and provides more flexibility on the page design.

- **Go for SPA (Single Page Application)**: SPA (for example, Gmail) provides a quicker and responsive navigational experience to the user. They are distinguished by their ability to redraw any part of the UI without requiring a server roundtrip to retrieve a page. While building mobile applications, go for SPA if it does not complicate your development process. Kendo UI Mobile is an excellent framework to build single page applications as you will see in the future chapters.

- **Make full use of offline mode and local data storage**: Almost all modern mobile browsers these days support quite a lot of the HTML5 specification, as their update frequency is very high as compared to their desktop counterparts. Although we can safely assume that these features will be available on the mobile browsers, it's a good idea to check whether these features are enabled on the client browser using simple JavaScript conditional statements.

Summary

In this chapter we discussed different ways of developing a mobile application and had an introduction with HTML5 and CSS3. We also got our hands dirty by writing some sample code in HTML5 and CSS3. It is important to understand the power of HTML5 and CSS3 combined, which will provide the most powerful tool for mobile application development for the next generation apps. Then we had a high-level look at Kendo UI architecture and finished off with some of the design guidelines for HTML5 mobile applications.

In the next chapter we will take a deep dive into Kendo UI Mobile, write some code, and develop few screens of an application which will be developed as a fully functional web application as we progress through this book.

2
Building Your First Mobile Application

In this chapter we will get our hands dirty, warm up with some Kendo UI Mobile code, and then kick start building an end-to-end mobile application called Movie Tickets. Over the course of the book, we will discover new features and enhance our application to make it a full-fledged, deployable mobile application! Initially we will treat this application as a single page application, which can be hosted on a web server or accessed by loading the index.html file locally on a browser, so as to ease the pain of debugging and testing.

Preparing the development machine

Setting up the environment for developing Kendo UI Mobile applications is simple and straightforward. Create a base HTML file, add the required .js and .css Kendo UI Mobile file references and you are ready to go. You will only require a text editor to develop Kendo UI applications unless you want to use an HTML IDE such as Visual Studio, Dreamweaver, or Komodo. The only external dependency for Kendo UI is jQuery. Always check the version of jQuery supported by the version of Kendo UI you are using. There is no guarantee that the latest version of jQuery will be supported by the latest version of Kendo. So the safest way is to use the jQuery file available with the Kendo UI package.

You can use any operating system with an HTML5-supported browser to develop Kendo UI Mobile applications. The process that we will follow in this book to develop the mobile app will be to do the development on a desktop machine and run it on an emulator and a mobile device as a mobile website. The IDE we will be using is Visual Studio 2012 and the emulator will be Ripple from **Research In Motion (RIM)**. If you are not comfortable using Visual Studio, feel free to use any HTML editor or a text editor; you will hardly feel any difference.

If you don't have Microsoft Visual Studio, a free copy of Visual Studio Express 2012 for web or a trial version of other flavors can be downloaded from this link: `http://www.microsoft.com/visualstudio/downloads`

Ripple Emulator

Mobile application development is different from desktop application development as the former is developed on a desktop and deployed on a mobile device, and the latter is developed and used on a desktop computer. Testing and debugging apps on mobile devices is not straightforward and sometimes close to impossible. As a result, emulators play a key role in testing and debugging mobile applications on desktops.

Ripple Emulator is one of the preferred emulators in the market which emulates a wide variety of mobile platforms such as Android, iOS, and BlackBerry. Ripple offers the ability to debug HTML5 mobile applications, giving full visibility into how the app will look in different platforms. Ripple helps developers to implement automated testing, JavaScript debugging, and multiple device and screen resolution emulation in real time without having to redeploy the mobile application or restart the emulator.

Ripple runs as a Google Chrome browser extension and so you will need to have Google Chrome installed on your machine.

Installing Ripple Emulator

The installation of Ripple is pretty straightforward and can be done in the following easy steps:

1. Install the Google Chrome browser if it's not already installed and navigate to the Google Chrome store: `https://chrome.google.com/webstore/`.

2. Search for **Ripple Emulator**.

3. Now click on the **ADD TO CHROME** button.

4. Click on **Add** when the following popup appear:

5. Ripple will now be installed on your Chrome browser and can be enabled/disabled using the Ripple icon that appears on the top-right corner of the browser:

6. Now let's visit the mobile website of `reuters.com` and see Ripple in action. Enter `http://mobile.reuters.com/` on the browser address bar and when the website loads, click on the **Enable** button. If Ripple asks to select a platform to test with, select a platform of your choice. I am selecting **Apache Cordova/PhoneGap** so that we can emulate the behavior of a mobile app bundled using Cordova/PhoneGap. Once inside the emulator, you can select a device from the **Devices** list on the left. Let's select **iPhone 5** and see how `reuters.com` appears on iPhone 5:

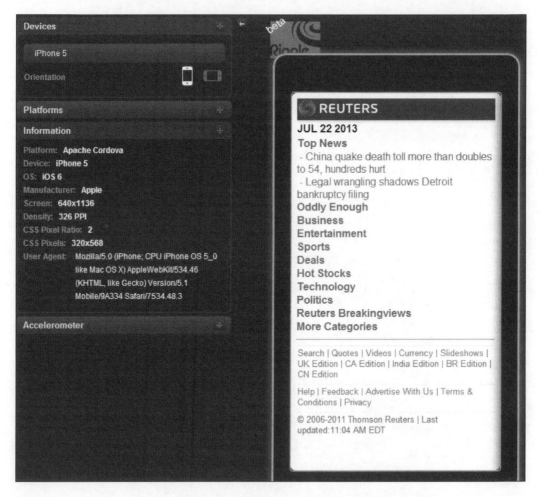

Ripple comes with lots of features such as changing device orientation, shaking the device, setting geolocation, and firing platform-specific events which helps developers to test and debug mobile applications on their desktop. We would highly recommend playing with Ripple Emulator a little bit at this point and getting a feel of all its features.

To test your mobile application locally using Ripple Emulator, it needs to be hosted as a website using your local web server. To learn more about Ripple, visit: `https://developer.blackberry.com/html5/documentation/getting_started_with_ripple_1866966_11.html`

Of course, nothing can replace the actual testing on mobile devices. In many cases, the Kendo UI Mobile styles look better on mobile devices than on desktop browsers. If you are serious about the application that you are developing, make sure you get your hands on all the target devices and do some rounds of testing before deploying the application.

First Kendo UI Mobile application

The best way to learn any new technology or language is to take a deep dive in to it and get your hands dirty. Since this book is all about more and more code, let's start by creating a simple, single page application.

We will follow a progressive enhancement approach starting with basic elements and adding more complexity to the application and, towards the end, we will create a fully functional deployable application.

 Kendo UI Mobile supports only WebKit browsers and so it's important to use Chrome or Safari browsers to run the demo code on your desktop.

Now that you have your IDE and emulator ready, perform the following steps to get your first mobile page running:

1. Download Kendo UI from the following URL: `http://www.kendoui.com/download.aspx`. You can either purchase a Kendo UI license or download a free 30-day trial version.

2. Create a `root` folder for the application and copy the following mobile-specific files/folders from the Kendo package to this folder:

   ° The `jquery.min.js` and `kendo.mobile.min.js` files from the `js` folder to the application root's `js/kendo` folder

   ° The `kendo.mobile.all.min.css` and `images` folders from the `styles` folder to the application root's `styles/kendo` folder

3. Create an `index.html` file in the `root` folder with the following code in it:

```html
<!DOCTYPE HTML>
<html>
  <head>
    <script src="js/kendo/jquery.min.js"> </script>
    <script src="js/kendo/kendo.mobile.min.js"></script>
    <link href="styles/kendo/kendo.mobile.all.min.css"
      rel="stylesheet" />
  </head>
  <body>
    <div data-role="view" data-title="Movie Tickets"
      id="mt-home-main-view" data-layout="mt-main-layout">
      Home Page View
    </div>
    <div data-role="layout" data-id="mt-main-layout">
      <header data-role="header">
        <div data-role="navbar">
        <span data-role="view-title">Movie Tickets</span>
        </div>
      </header>
      <footer data-role="footer">
        <span style="color:#fff">  Footer content goes here
          </span>
      </footer>
    </div>
    <script>
      var application = new kendo.mobile.Application();
    </script>
  </body>
</html>
```

Kendo hosts the minified versions of JS and CSS files required for development in a **Content Delivery Network (CDN)** which can be accessed as follows:

`http://cdn.kendostatic.com/`**`<version>`**`/`
`js/`**`<filename>`**`.min.js`

`http://cdn.kendostatic.com/`**`<version>`**`/`
`styles/`**`<filename>`**`.min.css`

For example:

`http://cdn.kendostatic.com/2013.2.716/`
`styles/kendo.mobile.all.min.css`

`http://cdn.kendostatic.com/2013.2.716/js/`
`kendo.mobile.min.js`

4. Configure your local web server so that `index.html` can be accessed using a URL; something like `http://localhost/movietickets/index.html`

> If you are unfamiliar with how to create a virtual directory in IIS, you can find it here: `http://goo.gl/0fUO1`. If you are using operating systems other than Windows, please get help from tons of manuals available on the Internet explaining how to host a website locally.
>
> Always remember that this step is required only if you need to test the mobile application using Ripple Emulator. You can always open your website in an HTML5 compatible browser such as Safari or Chrome and see your application running and use their debugging tools too.

> WebKit is an open source browser rendering engine which is used by browsers such as Safari and Chrome. So if you are targeting your app to be bundled using PhoneGap or any other WebKit-based mobile development framework, it's typically safe to test the app using any of the WebKit-based browsers as they share the same rendering engine.

5. Open Chrome and navigate to the `index.html` file we created earlier. Click on the Ripple's **Enable** button and select the device as the latest version of iPhone. If asked for a platform, feel free to select any of the platforms such as **PhoneGap**, or **Mobile Web**. We are selecting **Apache Cordova/ PhoneGap(1.0.0)** and **iPhone 5** (**PhoneGap 2.0.0** version in Ripple may cause the screen to scroll which is not the desired behavior).

Congratulations, your first mobile app using Kendo UI Mobile is up and running!

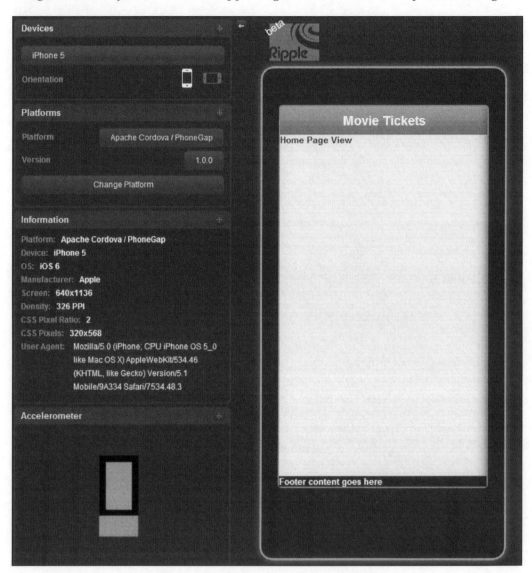

 If you are planning to bundle your mobile app using a native wrapper such as Cordova/PhoneGap, always bundle the required script files locally and avoid CDNs as this will delay the load time of our application considerably.

Views and Layouts

A view widget represents a page in a Kendo UI Mobile application. All widgets and other HTML elements are added inside a view. Any Kendo UI Mobile app will have one or more views.

A `data-role` attribute is used to define what particular mobile widget the HTML element will become once it is rendered.

The attribute definition `data-role="view"` defines a view and the `data-layout` attribute is used to define which template will act as the layout for our view as shown in our previous example:

```
<div data-role="view" id="mt-home-main-view"
    data-layout="mt-main-layout"> Home Page View </div>
```

A layout is nothing but a master wrapper into which a view will be rendered.

When a view is initialized, all Mobile, Web, and DataViz widgets in the view are initialized in that order.

In the earlier code, we have declared two other roles, header and footer, inside the layout which will render as header and footer of the view respectively.

 An important point to be noted is that since Kendo UI Mobile is designed so that the apps automatically adapt to the native look and feel of the mobile platform on which it runs, the position of the header and footer is reversed for Android and iOS devices due to OS UI design conventions. In iOS, the header is displayed on top and the footer at the bottom of the screen, while the same code in an Android device will display the footer on top and the header at the bottom.

NavBar

The next widget that we encounter is defined as `data-role = "navbar"`, which as its definition suggests is the NavBar or the Navigation Bar widget in which we can add a title and/or other widgets. We will see how other widgets are added to the navigation bar soon, but right now we are only adding the title of the application.

Typically NavBar is added in layouts and so depending on the view loaded, the title of the NavBar needs to change. Kendo provides an easy way of doing this.

Just add an HTML element with the attribute `data-role="view-title"` inside the NavBar. When the view changes, the value set as the title of the view (using the `data-title` attribute of the view) will be automatically displayed in the NavBar inside the element decorated with the `view-title` role:

```
<!-- navbar definition -->
<div data-role="layout" data-id="my-layout">
  <div data-role="navbar">
  <span data-role="view-title">My View Title</span>
  </div>
</div>

<!-- view 1 -->
<div data-role="view" data-layout="my-layout"
  data-title="View 1 Title"></div>

<!-- view 2 -->
<div data-role="view" data-layout="my-layout"
  data-title="View 2 Title"></div>
```

Application initialization

The HTML code that we discussed earlier contains definitions of widgets only and to bring them to life, we need to initialize our app as a Kendo UI Mobile app. This is done using a small magical piece of code:

```
var application = new kendo.mobile.Application();
```

This piece of code initializes your Kendo UI Mobile application and gives life to all the widgets and it needs to be added just before the `</body>` tag.

The application initialization script is very powerful and can be extended to set a lot of global properties of the application which we will explore later in the chapter.

> All Kendo UI Web widgets are highly touch optimized and designed to run on mobile devices too. So you can always use a Web widget inside a mobile application if the need arises.

A real-world mobile app – Movie Tickets

Now let's get to the real deal and develop a fully functional mobile app using Kendo UI Mobile and see how it can be integrated with a RESTful service (ASP.NET Web API in our case which will be introduced in *Chapter 3, Service Layer with ASP.NET Web API*).

Before we start building our Movie Tickets application, let's quickly go through the screens and functionalities that will be implemented in the app at a high-level:

- User can search for a particular movie and then select a theater for a show.

- Once user selects a show time, application asks the user for number of tickets and displays the rate. The total amount will be automatically updated once the number of tickets is entered.

- After booking, user can see completed bookings in the booking history view.

- In the user account screen, user can update name, e-mail ID, address, and so on.

- In the trailers tab, video trailers are displayed which can be navigated using the swipe gesture.

The Home screen

Now let's build the home screen of our mobile application using the single screen application that we've developed. We will add a tab strip in the footer of the screen, so that the contents in the middle can scroll and the tab strip remains static. In the tab strip we will add tabs such as **Movies**, **Trailers**, **My Account**, and **About**. We will then create views for these screens and navigate to the respective view when the link on the tab strip is clicked.

The completed Movie Tickets application will look like this:

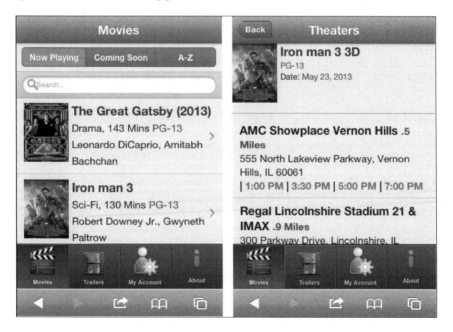

You can see the booking and trailers page in the following screenshot:

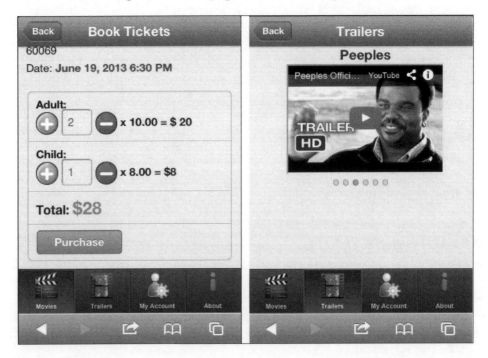

The TabStrip widget

The Kendo UI Mobile framework ships with lots of useful widgets which helps to build great looking apps quickly. We will take a quick look at the TabStrip widget here, as it is one of the most important widgets in the framework, and we will explore other widgets in *Chapter 5, Exploring Mobile Widgets* in detail.

The TabStrip widget is used to display a group of navigation buttons usually in a layout footer element. On the click of the navigation buttons, respective views will be loaded.

When navigated to another view, it updates the TabStrip's currently selected tab, based on the current view's URL. The TabStrip comes with built-in tab icons which can be used by setting the data-icon attribute to the anchor element or we can add other images by adding an img tag inside the anchor element.

Here is the list of all built-in icons provide by Kendo:

about	favorites	pause
action	featured	play
add	toprated	recents
bookmarks	globe	refresh
camera	history	reply
cart	home	rewind
compose	info	search
contacts	more	settings
details	mostrecent	share
downloads	mostviewed	stop
fastforward	organize	trash

Let's open up the view that we created before and add the following code to the footer after replacing the current footer contents:

```
<footer data-role="footer">
  <div data-role="tabstrip">
    <a href="#mt-home-main-view">
      <img src="images/movies.ico"
      height="40" width="40" /><br />
      Movies
    </a>

    <a href="#mt-about-view" data-icon="about">
      <br />
      About
    </a>
  </div>
</footer>
```

Now copy the images folder from the source code folder of the book to your workspace's root so that all the images we are using will be visible to you.

Here we have used a custom icon and a built-in icon as the navigation buttons. The href attribute has the values of view IDs prepended with #. This tells the application that when this button is clicked, we need to navigate to a particular view.

Navigation between views in the same file is the basic level of navigation and soon we will see how navigation to external URLs, remote views (views in external files), and data transfer in query string can be done.

Clicking on the **Movies** navigation button will take you to the home page of the app and a click on the **About** icon will take you to the **About** view which we will add as shown just after the closing div of the first view:

```
<!-- about view -->
<div data-role="view" id="mt-about-view" data-title="About"
  data-layout="mt-main-layout">
  <div style="padding: 15px">
    This is a sample application developed for the book
    Building Mobile Applications using Kendo UI Mobile
      and ASP.NET Web API
  </div>
</div>
```

The code is pretty self-explanatory. A new view with the same layout is added for the **About** view in the same file.

The two screens will look like this when viewed using Ripple Emulator or an iPhone:

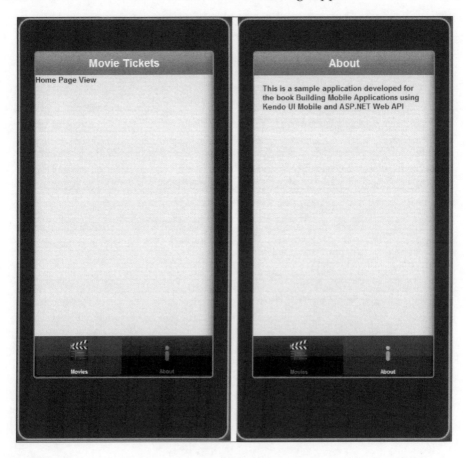

Transitions

Kendo offers different transition effects while navigating through views and if you need a single type of transition across the application, we can configure it in the app initialization script as shown here:

```
var application = new kendo.mobile.Application(document.body,
  {
  transition: 'fade'
});
```

Different transition effects supported by Kendo UI Mobile are:

- **zoom**: Current view fades out and the new view along with the header and footer zooms from the center of the screen.

- **slide**: This is the default transition. Transition direction can be specified by using `slide :(direction)`.Value of direction parameter can be `left` or `right`. Current view slides to the direction specified and the new view takes its place sliding in. If no direction parameter is specified, `left` is taken as the default direction parameter.

- **overlay**: The new view slides on top of the current view without transitioning the header and footer. The `overlay:(direction)` parameter can be used to specify transition direction and possible values are `left`, `right`, `up` and `down`. For example, `transition: 'overlay:up'`.

- **fade**: The new view along with its header and footer content fades in on the top of the current view content.

The parameter `reverse` can be specified along with the transition effect to play the transition in reverse. If we specify `slide:right reverse` in a view and try to navigate to the previous view, the previous view will slide in from the left.

Navigation

In the previous example, we have seen how navigation happens between local views (views within the same file) using the `href` attribute in the `anchor` tag. Now let's explore the navigation framework of Kendo UI Mobile in detail.

The Remote view

To keep all the views of an application within the same physical file is not practical while developing a big application with lots of screens. Almost always, developers will want to have each screen/module in its own HTML file, which will help in code maintenance and ease of development when a team of programmers are working on the application.

Handling this scenario is straightforward in Kendo UI Mobile. If we need to load a remote/external view, it is only required to specify the filename of the external view for navigation instead of the view's ID. When navigated to a remote view, Kendo UI Mobile loads the view using an Ajax call, caches the contents of the file, and displays the first view encountered in the file. If there are additional views in the file, they will be appended to the **Document Object Model (DOM)**, but will not be initialized or displayed. Any inline style/script elements and mobile layout definitions will also be evaluated and appended to the application.

To see this in action, let's create a file called `Trailers.html` in the `root` directory with the following contents:

```
<div data-role="view" data-title="Trailers"
  data-layout="mt-main-layout" id="mt-trailers-view">

</div>
```

As you can see, there is no need to add the Kendo reference files as these are already referred from the `index.html` file.

Now that we have an external view, let's navigate to this external view using our TabStrip widget. Open up `index.html` and a new navigation element between the **Search** and **Movies** buttons appears, as shown in the following code snippet:

```
<a href="Trailers.html">
  <img src="images/trailers.ico" height="40" width="40" /><br />
  Trailers
</a>
```

Now reload `index.html` in your emulator or on your mobile device and click on the **Trailers** icon and you can see that the view is loaded just like our local view:

When a remote view is loaded, styles/scripts from the `<head>` element, if any, will not be evaluated.

> There could be use cases where you need to navigate to an external URL and for this, just add the `data-rel="external"` attribute to the navigation element. Keep in mind that this will load the external URL on the browser by unloading your app and you will be at the mercy of your device or the browser's back button to return to your application.

The Back button

The back button is one of the most widely used UI elements of a mobile application and is typically added to the top navigation bar. Kendo UI Mobile provides us with a back button widget which is very easy to use; just add `data-role="backbutton"` on an `anchor` tag and our back button is ready! Kendo UI Mobile handles back page navigation automatically, which is in-built with the back button widget.

Adding the markup for the back button to our application's NavBar widget will display the back button on the top-left corner of all the three views we have built till now:

```
<header data-role="header">
  <div data-role="navbar">
    <a data-align="left" data-role="backbutton">Back</a>
    <span data-role="view-title">Movie Tickets</span>
  </div>
</header>
```

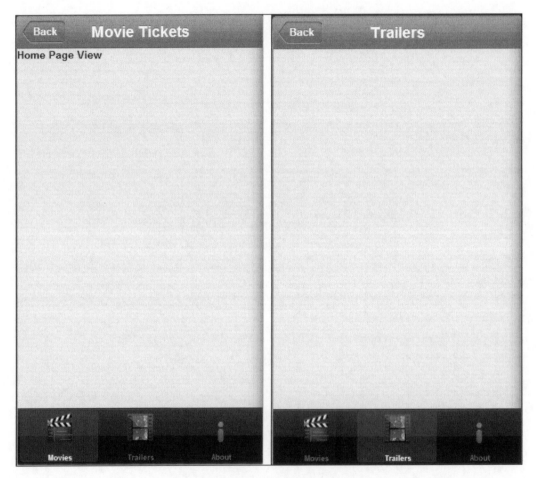

Now we have a problem to fix. The back button is displayed in all the views including the home view too, which is not required. Some mobile development frameworks such as jQuery Mobile automatically hide the back button on home screens, but in Kendo UI Mobile, we will have to handle it ourselves.

Again, this is very straightforward to implement. We need to update the home view definition and add a CSS class:

```
<div data-role="view" id="mt-home-main-view"
  data-show="homeViewInit" data-layout="mt-main-layout"
  class="no-backbutton">
  Home Page View
</div>
```

Let's add this CSS snippet to the <head> tag:

```
<style>
  .no-backbutton .km-back { visibility: hidden; }
</style>
```

Now if we run the application, we can see that the back button is not visible on the home page. The rendered back button will have a CSS class km-back added to it automatically by Kendo UI Mobile. The previous CSS snippet will hide the elements with the km-back CSS class inside the element with the CSS class no-backbutton, which is our home view.

Looking into the rendered HTML

One interesting fact to note here is that the layout header is rendered inside the view div and the rest of the contents in the view div are displayed after the header, inside the content element, and after that the footer elements are appended.

The rendered HTML can be investigated using Chrome/Safari developer tools:

```
▼<body class="km-on-ios km-ios km-ios5 km-5 km-m0 km-app km-pane km-vertical" data-role="pane" style>
  ▼<div data-role="view" id="mt-home-main-view" data-title="Movie Tickets" data-show="homeViewInit" data-layout="mt-main-
  layout" class="no-backbutton km-view" style>
    ▼<header data-role="header" class="km-header">
      ▼<div data-role="navbar" class="km-navbar">
        ▼<div class="km-leftitem">
          ▶<a data-align="left" data-role="backbutton" class="km-button km-back" href="#:back">…</a>
          </div>
        ▶<div class="km-view-title">…</div>
        </div>
      </header>
    ▼<div data-role="content" class="km-content km-scroll-wrapper" style="overflow: hidden;">
      <div class="km-scroll-header"></div>
      <div class="km-scroll-container" style="-webkit-transform-origin: 0% 0%;">
              Home Page View

        </div>
      <div class="km-touch-scrollbar km-horizontal-scrollbar" style="-webkit-transform-origin: 0% 0%; opacity: 0;"></div>
      <div class="km-touch-scrollbar km-vertical-scrollbar" style="-webkit-transform-origin: 0% 0%; opacity: 0;"></div>
      </div>
    ▼<footer data-role="footer" class="km-footer">
      ▼<div data-role="tabstrip" class="km-tabstrip">
        ▶<a href="#mt-home-main-view" class="km-button km-state-active" data-role="tab">…</a>
        ▶<a href="Trailers.html" class="km-button" data-role="tab">…</a>
        ▶<a href="#mt-about-view" data-icon="about" class="km-button" data-role="tab">…</a>
        </div>
      </footer>
    </div>
  <!-- about view -->
  ▶<div data-role="view" id="mt-about-view" data-title="About" data-layout="mt-main-layout" style="display: none;">…</div>
  ▶<script>…</script>
```

View loading and HTML element IDs

Now that we are comfortable creating multiple views and navigating to each other, it is important to understand how the views are loaded into the DOM, displayed, and how it is related to the HTML element IDs in views.

Let's consider the following navigation scenario in our sample application:

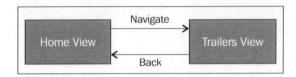

The user loads the application, views the home page, navigates to **Trailers** screen and then navigates back to the home page.

This is what happens in the DOM when the user does the earlier mentioned navigation:

- Layout and view for the home page is loaded.
- When the user navigates to the **Trailers** view, the view for the home page is made invisible using `style="z-index: 0; display: none;"`. Now the **Trailers** screen's view is loaded into the DOM and made visible. Then `z-index` of the view is set to 1.
- Now when the user navigates to the **Home** screen, the view of the **Trailers** screen is made invisible and the view of the **Home** screen is made visible and `z-index` is set to 1.

The important point to be noted is that once a view is loaded into the DOM, it is never removed; it's just made visible and invisible every time the user visits the view.

Let's inspect the DOM of our application after the user does the earlier mentioned navigation:

```html
▼<html lang="en" class="k-safari k-safari534 km-root km-phone">
  ▶<script id="tinyhippos-injected">…</script>
  ▶<head>…</head>
  ▼<body class="km-on-ios km-ios km-ios5 km-5 km-m0 km-app km-vertical km-pane" data-role="pane"
    style="overflow: auto;">
    ▼<div data-role="view" id="mt-home-main-view" data-title="Movie Tickets" data-show=
      "homeViewInit" data-layout="mt-main-layout" class="no-backbutton km-view" style="z-index: 1;">
      ▶<header data-role="header" class="km-header">…</header>
      ▶<div data-role="content" class="km-content km-scroll-wrapper" style>…</div>
      ▶<footer data-role="footer" class="km-footer">…</footer>
      </div>
      <!-- about view -->
    ▶<div data-role="view" id="mt-about-view" data-title="About" data-layout="mt-main-layout"
      style="display: none;">…</div>
    ▶<script>…</script>
    ▶<div class="km-loader" data-role="loader" style="display: none;">…</div>
    ▶<div data-role="view" data-title="Trailers" data-layout="mt-main-layout" id="mt-trailers-
      view" data-url="Trailers.html" class="km-view" style="z-index: 0; display: none;">…</div>
    </body>
</html>
```

We can see that the **Home** screen view's `z-index` is set to `1`, the **About** screen view is made invisible (this view is loaded as it is defined in `index.html`) and the **Trailers** view is made invisible with `z-index` set to `0`.

> Since the views, once initialized, always remain in the DOM and are just made visible and invisible, programmers must be careful with naming the HTML elements within views. If two views have elements with the same ID, and if any client-side code tries to access one of these elements using the same ID, it may cause unintended consequences. So it's advised to have proper naming convention for IDs, so that a conflict may not arise when multiple programmers are working on the code base. Prefixing all the element IDs with three or four characters of its view's name is one way of staying out of trouble!

Application object

Previously we have seen how to initialize the mobile application and set the transition configuration option. Transition is just one example from many global configurations that we can perform while instantiating a Kendo UI Mobile application. Let's explore some of the functionalities we can achieve using the Application object.

The Initial view

Using the initial configuration option, we can set the initial view to be displayed after the app is initialized:

```
new kendo.mobile.Application($(document.body), {
  initial: "intialViewID"
});
```

Loading text

Using the loading configuration we can set the text shown when the loading animation is displayed. If this value is set to `false`, loading animation will not be displayed. The text needs to be wrapped in <h1> </h1> tags:

```
new kendo.mobile.Application($(document.body), {
  loading: "<h1>Loading...</h1>"
});
```

Forcing platform

As we know, Kendo renders platform-specific UI. However, it provides the option to force a particular platform's look and feel on all the platforms using the platform configuration option:

```
<script>
  new kendo.mobile.Application($(document.body), {
    platform: "android"
  });
</script>
```

Even though this option is available, using a **Flat UI theme** is the recommended way of building apps with a consistent look and feel across platforms.

Hiding and showing the loading animation

The Application object helps to show and hide loading animation programmatically. The `showLoading()` method of the Application object displays the built-in loading animation of your Kendo Mobile app:

```
var application = new kendo.mobile.Application();
application.showLoading();
```

Using the `hideLoading()` method of the Application object, we can hide the loading animation.

```
var application = new kendo.mobile.Application();
application.hideLoading();
```

Getting a reference of the current view

When we develop a fully functional application, typically we will encounter a scenario where we need to get a reference of the currently displayed view in our JavaScript code.

The `view()` method of the Application object provides the reference of the currently displayed view object:

```
var application = new kendo.mobile.Application();
//writes title of the displayed view to the console.
  console.log(application.view().title);
```

Navigating to a view

In the previous examples we saw how we can navigate to other views declaratively. But what if you want to navigate to a screen using JavaScript? There is a solution for that too. The Application object that we created in our first example has a `navigate()` method, which can be used to perform navigation between views using JavaScript code. The method takes two parameters: URL to navigate, and transition effect (optional).

This is how we initialized our Kendo UI Mobile application:

```
var app = new kendo.mobile.Application();
```

Now we can make use of this object app to invoke the `navigate(url, transition)` method to navigate to another screen:

```
app.navigate("Trailers.html")
```

You can even use:

```
app.navigate("#mt-about-view", "slide")
```

 `navigate("#:back")` will take you back to the previously visited view.

UI experience across platforms

We've built the skeleton for our sample application and saw how the app looks on iOS. In *Chapter 1, Building a Mobile Application Using HTML5*, we've discussed Kendo's design philosophy of platform-specific look and feel. Now let's explore the Android experience and a Flat UI theme which provides a unified look and feel on all mobile platforms.

Let's experience the Android look and feel by changing the device to Nexus One in the Ripple Emulator:

As you can see, the look and feel of the app changed automatically when the app ran on an Android platform. Conforming to Android app design philosophy, the TabStrip widget is moved to the top and the **Back** button is displayed at the bottom.

This automatic look and feel is achieved by attaching platform-specific CSS classes to the rendered HTML. When the app is viewed in the Android platform, Android-specific CSS classes such as km-android are injected in to the <body> tag so that the elements inside <body> are decorated with classes tailored to the Android look and feel.

Let's see this in action by viewing our application in the Chrome developer tools' source view:

The same app when viewed on iPhone 5 will have an iOS-specific CSS attached:

The Flat view

Kendo provides an automatic platform-specific look and feel; well and good! But what if you would like to have a consistent look and feel across all platforms? Kendo has answered this question too with its 2013 Q2 release! Kendo UI Mobile now ships with a Flat UI theme, which is tailored around the iOS 7 UI design concepts. It provides a unified look and feel across all platforms. Once the Flat skin is enabled, you have only a set of CSS wrapped in the `km-flat` class to deal with for customization. This skin is particularly useful for enterprises that has colors associated with their brands and for apps which have their own trademark look and feel.

The Flat UI theme can be enabled by a simple configuration, `skin: 'flat'` while initializing the mobile application:

```
var application = new kendo.mobile.Application(document.body,
  {
      transition: 'slide',
      skin:'flat'
});
```

This is how our app looks on iPhone 5 and Nexus One phones with the Flat theme enabled:

Summary

In this chapter, we saw how to install and use the Ripple Emulator and how useful it can be for web developers while building mobile applications using Kendo UI Mobile. Then we created our first mobile application and started building our sample Movie Tickets application, and along with it learning the internals of Kendo UI Mobile. We also explored platform-specific UI rendering and the new Flat UI theme.

In the next chapter, we will learn how to build RESTful services using Microsoft's ASP.NET Web API. If you are a non .NET programmer, you can skip the next chapter and use the HTTP service hosted on the book's website.

3

Service Layer with ASP.NET Web API

In this chapter, ASP.NET Web API will be introduced with examples, and the service layer structure for our Movie Tickets application will be created. If you are not a .NET programmer or you don't intend to mess with data and service layers, feel free to skip this chapter. The service that we are building in this chapter is available online, which can be used while building the sample application. This service instance can be used as the backend, while following the Movie Tickets application integration. This chapter is not a complete reference of ASP.NET Web API, but details its features and how to use it to develop, service backend for our mobile client. An understanding of ASP.NET MVC is desired, but not necessary to follow the contents of this chapter.

In this chapter we will cover:

- Creating a Web API service
- Routing
- Parameter binding
- Building a service for the Movie Tickets application
- Content negotiation
- Securing Web API

ASP.NET Web API (formerly known as WCF Web API) is a framework that makes it easy to build resource-oriented services over HTTP, which can use the full features of HTTP and could be consumed by a wide variety of clients including browsers, console applications, services, mobile devices, and so on. It is an ideal platform for building **RESTful** applications on the .NET framework. Web API is shipped as part of ASP.NET MVC 4, which is available with Visual Studio 2012 and as an add-on for Visual Studio 2010 Service Pack 1.

ASP.NET Web API embraces HTTP as an application-level protocol, leverages the concepts of HTTP, and provides the following features:

- Built-in action mapping in controller, based on HTTP verbs (GET, POST, PUT, and so on)

- **Content negotiation**: Using this feature the service decides the format of the response based on the client's request

- Request/response body can consist of any type of content, such as binary files(image/audio/video...), HTML, JSON and so on; and not just XML content as required by SOAP

- **Host independent**: Can be hosted inside ASP.NET as well as self-hosted in our own host process

Creating a Web API service

Let's now open up Visual Studio 2012 and create the ASP.NET Web API backend service for our Movie Tickets app in C#.

Please note that the service layer that we are building in this chapter is available online at the following URL:

`http://api.kendomobilebook.com/api/`

The service methods available here can be used for testing and integrating with your app if you do not want to create the service locally.

Now, carry out the following steps to create the Web API service:

1. Make sure that you have installed Visual Studio 2012/2010 with MVC 4. If not installed, you can use the Microsoft Web Platform Installer to install them from the following link:

    `http://www.microsoft.com/web/downloads/platform.aspx`

2. Launch Visual Studio, create a new project by navigating to the **File** menu and then **New | Project...**. Now from the pop up menu, select Visual C# Template from the left menu and select the **ASP.NET MVC 4 Web Application** template. Name the project as `MovieTickets.WebAPI` and click on **OK**.

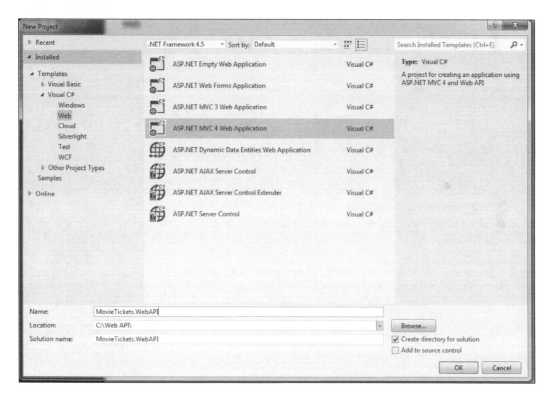

3. In the project pop-up window, as shown in the following, select the **Web API** template from the template list. If you are interested in writing unit tests for your Web API services, you can check the **Create a unit test project** checkbox and Visual Studio will automatically create a test project for you.

You can select any one of the templates from the list as they all will contain DLL files and configurations required to create Web API controllers. We selected the **Web API** template as this is the only template which comes with a sample Web API controller.

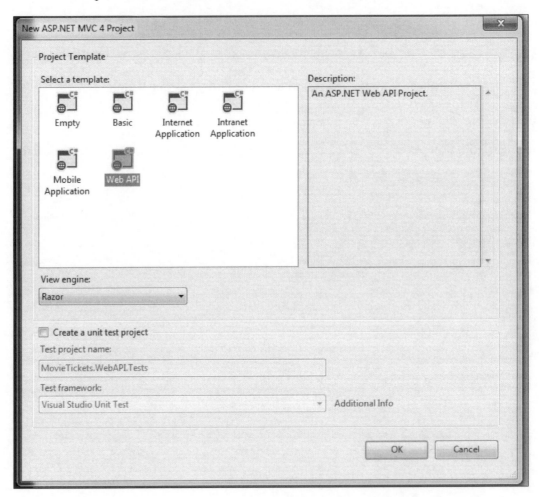

4. Our ASP.NET Web API service is now generated by Visual Studio with a host of MVC 4-related folders (**Content**, **Images**, **Scripts**, **Views**, and more), which can be removed from the project as we will be treating this solution only as an ASP.NET Web API service.

In the **Controllers** folder, two controllers are generated: HomeController.cs and ValuesController.cs. The first controller named HomeController.cs, is an MVC 4 controller and ValuesController.cs is a Web API controller. Along with other MVC 4 files and folders, the HomeController.cs file can also be removed from the project. The only file that is of interest for us right now is ValuesController.cs, which contains the ValuesController class and is a Web API controller, which is inherited from the base class ApiController unlike MVC controllers, which derives from the Controller base class.

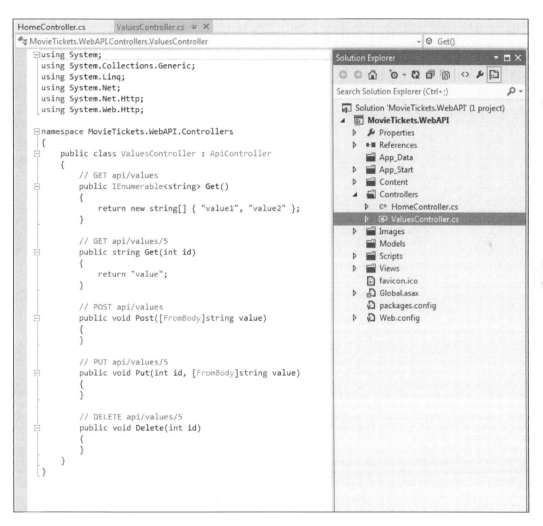

If we open up ValuesController.cs by clicking on it, we can see that Visual Studio has generated methods matching the HTTP verbs GET, POST, PUT, and DELETE, which are the typical actions performed by an HTTP request.

Hosting using IIS

Now that we have created our service, let's see it in action, hosted using ASP.NET runtime. Create an application in your local IIS on the folder in which our service resides (if you have **IIS Express** installed, you can use it too) so that the service can be accessed using the following URL on your machine:

```
http://localhost/movietickets.webapi
```

Depending on the version of IIS on your machine, the steps to do this may vary. On IIS 7, you can configure a new application using the following steps:

1. Build the solution by going to **BUILD | Build Solution** in Visual Studio.
2. Click the Windows **Start** button and in the **Run** textbox, type `inetmgr` and hit *Enter*.
3. Open IIS and right-click on **Default Web Site**.
4. Select **Add Application...** as shown in the following screenshot:

5. In the **Alias** field enter `MovieTickets.WebAPI`.

6. In the **Physical path** field, provide the physical path of the root directory of the project we created earlier.

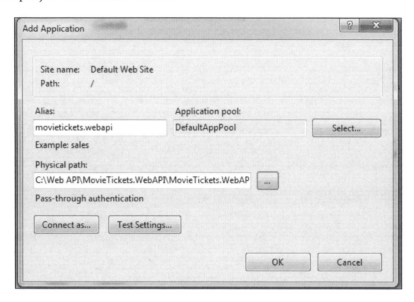

7. Click **OK** and our Web API service is ready to be used.

To test whether everything works fine, open up your favorite browser and hit the following URL in the address bar:

`http://localhost/movietickets.webapi/api/values`

An XML file will be shown on the browser with the data `value1` and `value2`, which was returned by the `GET` method in the `ValuesController` file as shown in the following screenshot:

Do not forget to add /api/ in the URL, otherwise you will get a 404 error. Here api is used only as a convenient way to avoid routing conflicts between MVC and Web API controllers in the same project. You can see how this works in the next section.

Routing

Routing, simply put, is the process of receiving a request and mapping it to a controller action. If you are familiar with MVC routing, you will find that Web API routing is similar to it but with some differences; Web API uses the HTTP request type instead of the action name in the URL (as in the case of MVC) to select the action to be executed in the controller.

Routing configuration for Web API is defined in the file App_Start\WebApiConfig. cs. The default routing configuration of ASP.NET Web API is as shown in the following:

```
namespace MovieTickets.WebAPI
{
    public static class WebApiConfig
    {
        public static void Register(HttpConfiguration config)
        {
            config.Routes.MapHttpRoute(
                name: "DefaultApi",
                routeTemplate: "api/{controller}/{id}",
                defaults: new { id = RouteParameter.Optional }
            );
        }
    }
}
```

The default routing template of Web API is api/{controller}/{id} as highlighted in the previous code.

If we open up the default routing configuration for MVC in the file App_Start\ RouteConfig.cs, we can see that the default routing definition is provided as {controller}/{action}/{id}.

```
namespace MovieTickets.WebAPI
{
    public class RouteConfig
    {
        public static void RegisterRoutes(RouteCollection routes)
        {
```

```
routes.IgnoreRoute("{resource}.axd/{*pathInfo}");

routes.MapRoute(
    name: "Default",
    url: "{controller}/{action}/{id}",
    defaults: new
    {
        controller = "Home",
        action = "Index",
        id = UrlParameter.Optional
    }
);
        }
    }
}
```

An obvious difference that can be noticed between the two route definitions is that in the Web API route definition, {action} route value is missing. This is because in Web API, the HTTP verb is used to locate the action and so the URI is not required to provide the action name.

As an example, when Web API receives a GET request for a particular controller, the list of matching actions are all methods whose name starts with GET (for example, GetMovies, GetTheaters, and so on). The same is the case with all the other HTTP verbs. The correct action method to be invoked is identified by matching the signature of the method.

This naming convention for action methods can be overridden by using the HttpGet, HttpPut, HttpPost, or HttpDelete attributes with the action methods. For example, we can rename the action method Get(int id) to MyValues(int id) and decorate it with an HttpGet attribute:

```
[HttpGet]
public string MyValues(int id)
{
    return "my value";
}
```

Now when we hit the browser with the URL http://localhost/movietickets. webapi/api/value/1, you can see that the string my value will be returned. If the attribute HttpGet is removed from the action, Web API will not identify the method MyValues as an action method.

Customizing the Web API routing

The default Web API routing is suitable for ideal scenarios where there are only a few action methods defined for each of the HTTP verbs and they vary only in their method signatures. Depending on your project requirements you could end up with a need to have multiple GET methods or multiple POST methods with different functionality and names, and the application that invokes these methods needs to call them by their names instead of allowing Web API to figure out the method name using the HTTP verb.

Let's see this scenario in action by adding another action method called GetMyValues to our ValuesController:

```
public string GetMyValues()
{
    return "Get my values";
}
```

Now the requirement is that we need to call this particular action method and let's try to do it by calling this method using this URL:

http://localhost/movietickets.webapi/api/values/GetMyValues

The result will be an error message as shown in this screenshot:

The message says **Multiple actions were found that match the request:**, which happens because Web API routing identifies two action methods matching this request; Get and GetMyValues.

To fix this, we need to add the following route configuration in the `WebApiConfig` class, which uses action name-based routing above the current configuration:

```
public static void Register(HttpConfiguration config)
    {
        config.Routes.MapHttpRoute(
            name: "DefaultApi2",
            routeTemplate: "api/{controller}/{action}/{id}",
            defaults: new { id = RouteParameter.Optional }
        );
    }
```

Make sure that you add this routing configuration *above* the Web API default configuration, otherwise the default route will take precedence and the **Multiple actions were found...** error will be displayed again.

Once the previous code is added and we hit the URL

`http://localhost/movietickets.webapi/api/values/Getmyvalues` again on the browser, we can see the new result:

```
▼<string xmlns="http://schemas.microsoft.com/2003/10/Serialization/">
  <script/>
  Get my values
</string>
```

Parameter binding

Parameter binding is all about converting contents in an HTTP request to .NET objects so that values can be provided to action method parameters. Without parameter binding support, developers will have to write lots of error-prone and tedious code in action methods to retrieve parameter values from raw HTTP requests.

Input parameters are typically embedded in an HTTP request in URI as query strings, or in the body of the request. Web API uses a technique called **Model Binding** to read parameter values from the query string, and uses **Formatters** to read from the request body.

Model binding

If you are familiar with ASP.NET MVC, then you'll find that it's the same Model Binding concept being used in Web API for reading values from query strings, headers, or body encoded with `application/form-url-encoded`. When a request is encountered, value providers registered in the `ValueProviderFactories` class extracts data from the request and provides them to a model binder, which creates model objects using these values.

By default, simple types such as `string`, `Date Time`, `Guid`, `decimal`, and other types decorated with a **type converter** use Model Binding.

The `[ModelBinder]` attribute can be used on the parameter or parameter's type to force Model Binding. The `[FromUri]` attribute derived from `[ModelBinder]` tells a model binder to only look in the URI for values.

Formatters

Web API uses Formatters to read data from the HTTP request body for parameter binding. Formatters were introduced in Web API to provide better Content Negotiation abilities. Content negotiation is a mechanism that allows a web server to serve content in different formats as requested by the client using the same URL, which will be discussed later in this chapter.

Media Formatters derive from the `MediaTypeFormatter` class. All the configured Formatters are available in the `HttpConfiguration.Formatters` collection. Web API identifies the correct Formatter to be used from this collection using the content type of the incoming request.

The request body content in ASP.NET Web API is treated as forward-only, read once, and non-buffered stream. This means:

- We can have only one `complex` type in the action method signature. If more than one `complex` type is required, all the others except one must be decorated with the `[ModelBinder]` attribute.
- If a Formatter was used to read parameter values from the request body, then the request body will not be accessible any more in the action methods.

This is a major difference from MVC's parameter binding, where the request body is buffered so that it could be searched multiple times for parameter values.

Web API provides Formatters for XML and JSON out of the box, and developers can create custom Formatters to support other media types.

We can use the [FromBody] attribute to specify that a parameter should be read from the body rather than from the URI. This attribute is useful in scenarios where a simple type is sent as a parameter for a POST request. Web API, by default, will look in the URI for a simple type and since the request is a POST, the value will be in the body of the request.

In the ValuesController, the Post action method has the implementation of the [FromBody] attribute:

```
public void Post([FromBody] string value)
{
}
```

Building a service for the Movie Tickets application

Now that we have covered some of the basics of ASP.NET Web API, let's start building the backend service for our Movie Tickets application. Since this book is not about database or accessing data, the approach we are following is to hardcode data (data for objects are added while instantiating objects) that is returned by the service in a repository class and not to read the data from a database.

Let's look at the high-level view of our service architecture:

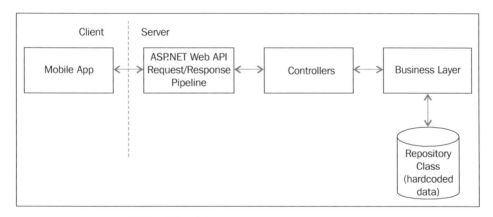

The service architecture is simplified so that we don't spend a lot of time on topics outside the context of the book, such as DB design, data access, and so on.

The requests from the client mobile app will be received by the ASP.NET Web API request pipeline and an action method in a controller will be invoked. The action method will, in turn, invoke the **Business layer** for fetching or updating data, which, in turn, invokes the **Repository class** to return **hardcoded data**. We will be discussing the creation of only one controller and action method in this chapter. The sample application and all other controllers and methods can be found in the code bundle available on Packt's website with the folder name as `chapter 3`. This approach helps in avoiding redundant code with no new information and helps us concentrate on the important topics of the book.

Follow these steps to set up the data for the list of movies, which will be displayed in the home page of our Movie Tickets application:

1. Create a file called `MovieBO.cs` in the `BLL\BusinessObjects` folder, and create a class called `MovieBO`, as shown in the following code:

```
public class MovieBO
{
    public int MovieId { get; set; }
    public string Name { get; set; }
    public string Rating { get; set; }
    public string Length { get; set; }
    public string Genre { get; set; }
    public string LeadStars { get; set; }
    public string Image { get; set; }
    public bool IsNowPlaying { get; set; }
}
```

2. Create a class called `MovieRepository` in the file `BLL\ MovieRepository. cs`, which is responsible for generating data which our service will return to the client. After adding the new class, add a class-level `public static` variable called `moviesMasterList`:

```
public static List<MovieBO> moviesMasterList;
```

This variable will hold a master list of movies and the business logic will query this collection to select matching its queries.

3. Now let's add a method called `CreateMoviesMasterList` to add a couple of movies to the `moviesMasterList` variable:

```
private static void CreateMoviesMasterList()
{
    moviesMasterList = new List<MovieBO>()
    {
        new MovieBO(){
            MovieId = 1,
            Name = "The Great Gatsby (2013)",
```

```
                Genre = "Drama",
                Image = "http://images.kendomobilebook.com/movies/
        greatgatsby.jpg",
                IsNowPlaying = true,
                LeadStars = "Leonardo DiCaprio, Amitabh Bachchan",
                Length = "143",
                Rating = "PG-13"
            },
            new MovieBO(){
                MovieId = 2,
                Name= "Iron man 3",
                Genre= "Sci-Fi",
                Image = "http://images.kendomobilebook.com/movies/
        ironman3.jpg",
                IsNowPlaying = true,
                LeadStars = "Robert Downey Jr., Gwyneth Paltrow",
                Length = "130",
                Rating = "PG-13"
            }
        };
    }
```

4. Now create a public static method called `GetMoviesMasterList` to return the master list of movies:

    ```
    public static List<MovieBO> GetMoviesMasterList()
    {
        if (moviesMasterList == null
            || moviesMasterList.Count == 0)
        {
            CreateMoviesMasterList();
        }
        return moviesMasterList;
    }
    ```

5. For the sake of layered architecture, let's create a business layer, which is nothing but a class called `MovieTicketsBLL` in the `BLL\ MovieTicketsBLL. cs` file, which will contain static methods to access the repository and return business objects to the controller. Let's add a method called `GetMovies`, which will return movies as per the provided search string. If the search string is empty, the entire list of movies is returned:

    ```
    public static List<MovieBO> GetMovies(string searchKeyword)
    {
    var moviesMasterList = MovieRepository.GetMoviesMasterList();

        if (!string.IsNullOrEmpty(searchKeyword))
        {
            return (from m in moviesMasterList
    ```

```
                    where m.Name.StartsWith(searchKeyword,
            StringComparison.CurrentCultureIgnoreCase)
            select m
            ).ToList();
    }else
    {
        return moviesMasterList;
    }
}
```

Adding a controller

Now, we need to create a Web API controller called `MovieController`, which contains movie-related action methods.

Right-click on the **Controllers** folder, select **Add**, and then **Controller...**. In the **Add Controller** pop up, select **API controller with empty read/write actions** from the **Template** drop-down menu, and name it as `MoviesController`. Make sure that you don't select any of the MVC controller templates and select only the API controller template.

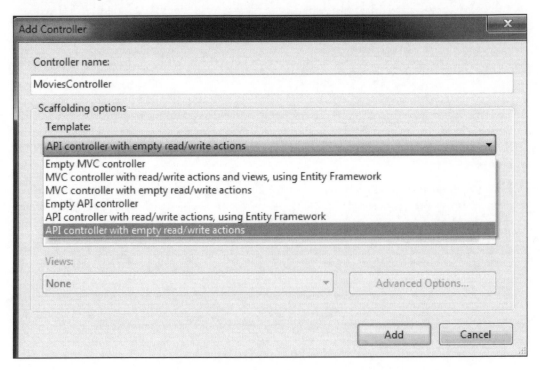

Once the controller file is generated, in the GET method, add the following code:

```
public List<MovieBO> Get(string id)
{
return MovieTicketsBLL.GetMovies(id);

}
public List<MovieBO> Get()
{
return MovieTicketsBLL.GetMovies("");
}
```

The first GET method will be invoked if there is a keyword to be searched that is passed along with the request. This action method will retrieve all the movies starting with the search keyword. If there is no input parameter, then the second GET method will be invoked, which will return the entire movies list. After adding the code, do refer to the namespaces under which the business object and the business layer is defined.

You are now ready to test your Web API method, which will return the list of movies as per your search criteria.

Shown here are the URLs used to invoke the Web API service and the results seen on the browser:

- To filter by movie names, insert the following URL in your browser address bar and hit *Enter*:

  `http://localhost/movietickets.webapi/api/movies/get/i`

- To see the entire movies list use the following URL and hit *Enter*:

  ```
  http://localhost/movietickets.webapi/api/movies/
  ```

Content Negotiation

You would have noticed by now that all our examples had data from the Web API service in XML format. Typically, while building mobile web applications, JSON is the preferred format and sometimes we may need to use either of these formats or some other custom formats. Thanks to Web API's **Content Negotiation** feature, clients can tell Web API services what content format it accepts, and Web API can serve the client with the same format automatically; provided that the format is configured in Web API. It supports XML and JSON formats only out of the box.

JSON is the preferred data interchange format these days because of the following reasons:

- JSON is lightweight and bandwidth non-intensive.

- JavaScript can directly consume JSON and parse it to JS objects. No format conversion is required.

- Growing interest in JSON-based horizontally scalable databases such as MongoDB, CouchDB and so on.

- JSON is interoperable with pretty much any programming language as it limits itself to primitive datatypes.

> W3C in its HTTP specification defines Content Negotiation as: the mechanism for selecting the appropriate representation for a given response when there are multiple representations available. See the following link for example:
> `http://www.w3.org/Protocols/rfc2616/rfc2616.txt`

Web API uses the `Accept`, `Content-Type` and `Accept-Charset` HTTP headers for Content Negotiation.

Using the `MoviesController` file, which we built in the previous section, let's see this in action.

The Advanced Rest Client Chrome extension

Advanced Rest Client is an extension available for chrome browsers, which is used to create and test custom HTTP requests. It supports features such as JSON/XML response viewer, socket debugging, setting custom headers, and more. We will explore the Content Negotiation feature of Web API using this simple and lightweight tool.

It can be installed on your Chrome browser from the following link:

`http://goo.gl/EdqIW`

If you're comfortable using web debugging tools such as **Fiddler**, feel free to use it as what we are trying to do here is to create some custom HTTP requests and compare the responses.

The Accept header

The HTTP Accept header is used to specify those media types that are acceptable to the client for the responses. For XML, the value is set as application/xml and for JSON it is application/json, and to specify that all media types are accepted */* is used.

To see this in action, let's open up the Advanced Rest Client extension and send a GET request to the URL http://localhost/movietickets.webapi/api/movies/get/i, and set the Add new header field to **Accept** header as application/json.

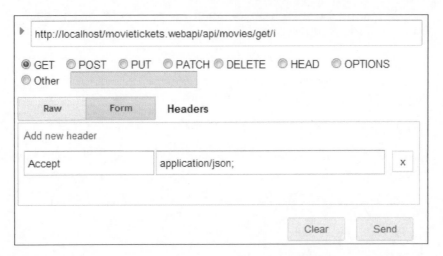

And the response from our Web API service can be seen in the following screenshot:

```
[1]
  -0:  {
     MovieId: 2
     Name: "Iron man 3"
     Rating: "PG-13"
     Length: "130"
     Genre: "Sci-Fi"
     LeadStars: "Robert Downey Jr., Gwyneth Paltrow"
     Image: "http://images.kendomobilebook.com/movies/ironman3.jpg"
     IsNowPlaying: true
  }
```

If you change the **Accept** header's value to application/xml, the response will be sent as XML by the Web API service as previously shown in the browser window.

The Content-type header

The Content-Type header in a request specifies the MIME type of the request body. When the Content-Type header is set (for POST and PUT requests) and the **Accept** header is not set, Web API will use the Content-Type header to decide the media type of the response.

If both the Accept and Content-Type headers are set, the media type specified in the Accept header is used to determine the media type of response. In this case, if a Formatter is not available in Web API for the media type defined in the Accept header, the Content-Type header will be chosen to determine the response media type.

The Accept-charset header

The Accept-Charset header is used to indicate the character encoding of the response unlike Accept and Content-Type headers, which specifies the MIME type of the response.

Web API uses both UTF-8 and UTF-16 character encoding out of the box, and by default UTF-8 is used. Setting Accept-Charset: utf-16 in the request header will return the response in UTF-16 encoding. To customize character encoding on the server-side on a per-Formatter basis, you need to change the SupportEncodings property on the MediaTypeFormatter class.

> If the request contains an **X-Requested-With** header, indicating an Ajax request, the server might default to JSON if there is no Accepted header specified.

> As mentioned earlier, Web API by default supports only XML and JSON media Formatters. To support other media types, developers need to create **Custom Formatters** by deriving from the MediaTypeFormatter (asynchronous read/write) class or the BufferedMediaTypeFormatter (synchronous read/write) class. Since the creation of custom Formatters is outside the scope of this book, we are not discussing this in detail here. If you are interested in exploring custom Formatters, this article by Mike Wasson will be a good starting point:
>
> http://goo.gl/moSOG

An Image/PDF file as response

It's a common requirement in most of the applications to retrieve a PDF or image file as response. It's quite easy to implement this scenario in Web API by writing a couple of lines of code in your action method to override the default media type of the response determined by Content Negotiation.

Let's open up the ValuesController.cs file, and add one more action method called GetImage(), which will return an image file in the Content folder of the service as shown:

```
public HttpResponseMessage GetImage()
{
    byte[] bytes = System.IO.File.ReadAllBytes(
        HttpContext.Current.Server
        .MapPath("~/Content/Kendo.png"));
    var result = new HttpResponseMessage(HttpStatusCode.OK);
    result.Content = new ByteArrayContent(bytes);
    result.Content.Headers.ContentType
        = new MediaTypeHeaderValue("image/png");

    return result;
}
```

Also refer to these two namespaces in the controller:

```
System.Web;
System.Web.Http;
```

The key to this implementation is the use of the HttpResponseMessage class, which helps to create a raw HTTP response in the controller itself. We then set the HTTP 200 status code using the enum HttpStatusCode.OK and set the image bytes as response content. The last step is to set the media type header to image/png, and the response is returned as HttpResponseMessage type.

Now hitting the URL http://localhost/movietickets.webapi/api/values/GetImage on your browser, this action method will display the elegant Kendo UI logo (if you had used the image which came with the source code!).

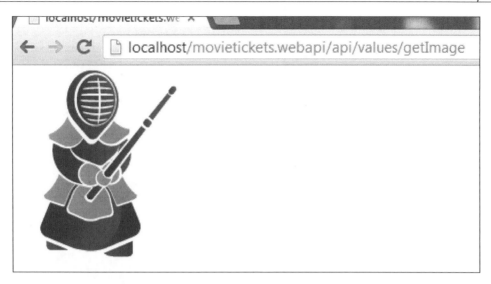

If the content is a PDF file, the only change we need to do is to update the MIME type as `application/pdf`.

Securing Web API

In real-world scenarios, most of the services that are published must be secured, and only authenticated clients should be able to access the services. The use of SSL in achieving transport layer security is, by default, implemented in almost all enterprise scenarios to prevent eavesdropping of the data travelling over the network. In this section, let's focus on the application-level security, by implementing **authentication** and **authorization**.

Authentication is the process of establishing that a user is who he claims to be and authorization is verifying whether the authenticated user can perform a particular action or consume a particular resource.

Authentication

By authentication, what we are trying to achieve is to make sure that every request received by the Web API service is sent from a client with proper credentials. There are different ways of implementing authentication such as Basic, Digest, and so on. We will be discussing Basic authentication, where the client sends a **Base64 encoded** username and password in the HTTP header for every request. Once you understand how to implement Basic authentication in Web API, it will be very easy to hook other forms of authentication as only the authentication process will be different and Web API hooks, where it is done, will be the same.

Basic authentication

Basic authentication, as its name suggests, is the most simple and basic form of authenticating HTTP requests. It doesn't require server-side session storage or implementation of cookies.

The following diagram shows the implementation of Basic authentication:

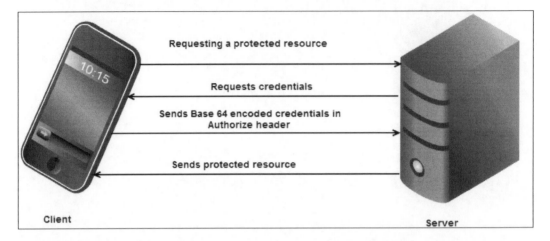

Authentication using message handlers

Web API expects its host (in our case, IIS) to authenticate requests. For this, we may have to use any of the ASP.NET authentication modules or write an HTTP module for implementing the authentication.

To authenticate an incoming request, the host needs to create a principal, which is an object of type IPrincipal that represents the current security context. Then the host needs to attach this principal object to the current thread by setting Thread. CurrentPrincipal. The Identity object associated with the principal has a property called IsAuthenticated. If the user is authenticated, this property will return true; otherwise it will return false. Since we are doing web hosting in our example project, we need to set the HttpContext.Current.User too, to make the security context consistent.

Typically, keeping authentication outside of the service is not what developers would like to have because of a variety of reasons. To keep the authentication piece within our service, we need to leverage Web API **message handlers**. Message handlers are derived from the abstract class `HttpMessageHandler`. They are responsible for receiving HTTP requests and sending responses. We can create custom message handlers by deriving from `System.Net.Http.DelegatingHandler`, and add our own raw HTTP data manipulation code. Deriving from `DelegatingHandler` helps to call the inner message handlers in the pipeline by calling `base.SendAsync`. In message handlers, requests are available as `HttpRequestMessage` and responses are available as `HttpResponseMessage`. When using handlers, the previous authentication process can be done easily using the `HttpRequestMessage` object.

These are the steps involved in doing Basic authentication using a custom message handler:

- Capture the incoming request using the message handler
- If the request contains an authorization header:
    - Try to authenticate the user and if authentication succeeds, set the principal and allow execution to continue
    - If the authentication fails, set HTTP status code 401 and return **WWW-Authenticate: Basic** in the response header

> **WWW-Authenticate: Basic** header is used to indicate that the authentication scheme used by this service is Basic.

Implementing authentication

Let's write some code and set up the authentication module for our Movie Tickets Web API project:

1. Create a folder called `Common`, add a class called `MovieTicketsPrincipal`, and add the following code:

```
using System.Security.Principal;

namespace MovieTickets.WebAPI.Common
{
    public class MovieTicketsPrincipal: IPrincipal
    {
        public string UserName { get; set; }
        public IIdentity Identity { get; set; }
        public bool IsInRole(string role)
```

```
        {
            if (role.Equals("user"))
            {
                return true;
            }
            else
            {
                return false;
            }
        }
        //Constructor
        public MovieTicketsPrincipal(string userName)
        {
            UserName = userName;
            Identity = new GenericIdentity(userName);
        }


    }
}
```

2. Create a folder called `Handlers` in the Movie Tickets Web API project, add a class called `AuthMessagehandler`, and add the following code:

```
using System;
using System.Net;
using System.Net.Http;
using System.Net.Http.Headers;
using System.Text;
using System.Threading;
using System.Web;
using MovieTickets.WebAPI.Common;

namespace MovieTickets.WebAPI.Handlers
{
    public class AuthMessagehandler : DelegatingHandler
    {

        private string _userName;

        //Capturing the incoming request by overriding
        //the SendAsync method
        protected override
            System.Threading.Tasks.Task<HttpResponseMessage>
            SendAsync(
            HttpRequestMessage request,
```

```
        CancellationToken cancellationToken)
    {
        //if the credentials are validated,
        //set CurrentPrincipal and Current.User
        if (ValidateCredentials(
            request.Headers.Authorization))
        {
            Thread.CurrentPrincipal
                = new MovieTicketsPrincipal(_userName);
            HttpContext.Current.User
                = new MovieTicketsPrincipal(_userName);
        }

        //Execute base.SendAsync to execute default
        //actions and once it is completed,
        //capture the response object and add
        //WWW-Authenticate header if the request
        //was marked as unauthorized.
        return base.SendAsync(request, cancellationToken)
            .ContinueWith(task =>
                {
                    HttpResponseMessage response
                        = task.Result;
                    if (response.StatusCode
                        == HttpStatusCode.Unauthorized
                        && !response.Headers
                        .Contains("WWW-;Authenticate"))
                    {
                        response.Headers
                            .Add("WWW-Authenticate", "Basic");
                    }
                    return response;
                });
    }


//Method to validate credentials from Authorization
//header value
    private bool ValidateCredentials(
        AuthenticationHeaderValue authenticationHeaderVal)
    {
        if ( authenticationHeaderVal!= null &&
            !String.IsNullOrEmpty(authenticationHeaderVal.
            Parameter))
        {

            string[] decodedCredentials
                = Encoding.ASCII.GetString(
```

```
                        Convert.FromBase64String(
                        authenticationHeaderVal.Parameter))
                        .Split(new[] { ':' });

//now decodedCredentials[0] will contain
//username and decodedCredentials[1] will
//contain password.You need to implement your own
//business logic to verify credentials here.
//For simplicity, we are hardcoding username
//and password here.

            if (decodedCredentials[0].Equals("username")
                && decodedCredentials[1].Equals("password"))
            {
                _userName = "John Doe";
                return true;//request authenticated.
            }
        }
        return false;//request not authenticated.
    }
  }
}
```

In this custom message handler, we are overriding the `SendAsync` method to capture the incoming request using the following code:

```
protected override System.Threading.Tasks.
Task<HttpResponseMessage> SendAsync(
        HttpRequestMessage request,
        CancellationToken cancellationToken)
    { }
```

Once the incoming request is captured, the `ValidateCredentials()` method is called to check HTTP headers for an `Authorization` header value which contains the username and password in a Base64 encoded format. If the header is found, the username and password are extracted and verified. In the previous code, we are verifying against hardcoded strings `username` and `password` for simplicity, but typically in real-world examples, the credentials will be checked against an active directory or a database. If the credentials are found to be correct, an object of type `MovieTicketsPrincipal` is created and assigned to `Thread.CurrentPrincipal` and `HttpContext.Current.User`. Now from anywhere in the service layer, the current user's details can be accessed for authorization, auditing, and so on. Once the response is authenticated, `base.SendAsync` is called to send the request to the inner handler. The request is processed and a response is sent back by the inner handler asynchronously.

The following code makes sure that the inner code is executed only after the response is received:

```
base.SendAsync(request, cancellationToken)
.ContinueWith(task =>{--- });
```

If the response contains an HTTP unauthorized header, the code injects a `WWW-Authenticate` header with the value `Basic` to inform the client that our service expects Basic authentication. More details about the request being marked as unauthorized will be discussed in the *Authorization* section.

3. Now open `Global.asax.cs` and add the following code in the `Application_Start` event as the first line:

```
GlobalConfiguration.Configuration
                .MessageHandlers.Add(new
AuthMessagehandler());
```

This code will add our `AuthMessagehandler` class to the `MessageHandlers` collection so that it gets called when a request arrives.

Authentication in action

To see our authentication mechanism in action, let's create a new request to the URL `http://localhost/movietickets.webapi/api/movie` with header **Authorization: Basic dXNlcm5hbWU6cGFzc3dvcmQ=** (where "dXNlcm5hbWU6cGFzc3dvcmQ=" is nothing but the Base64 encoded form of `username:password`) using Advanced REST Client, as shown in the following screenshot:

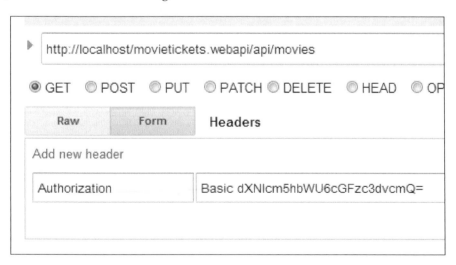

Now let's add a couple of break points in the `SendAsync` method and see the control flow:

```
            HttpRequestMessage request,
            CancellationToken cancellationToken)
    {
            //if the credentials are validated, set CurrentPrincipal and Current.User
            if (ValidateCredentials(request.Headers.Authorization))
            {            ⊞ ● request {Method: GET, RequestUri: 'http://localhost/movietickets.webapi/api/movies'
                Thread.CurrentPrincipal = new MovieTicketsPrincipal(_userName);
                HttpContext.Current.User = new MovieTicketsPrincipal(_userName);
            }
```

Now let's check the values of **Parameter** and **Scheme** properties by opening the request object:

```
    CancellationToken cancellationToken)
{
    //if the credentials are validated, set CurrentPrincipal and Current.User
    if (ValidateCredentials(request.Headers.Authorization))
    {                            ⊟ ⚲ request.Headers.Authorization {Basic dXNlcm5hbWU6cGFzc3dvcmQ=}
        Thread.CurrentPrincipal = new MovieTickets    ⚲ Parameter       🔍 ▾ "dXNlcm5hbWU6cGFzc3dvcmQ="
        HttpContext.Current.User = new MovieTicket    ⚲ Scheme          🔍 ▾ "Basic"
    }                                                ⊞ ● Non-Public members

    //Execute base SendAsync to execute default actions and once it is completed
```

As you can see, the credentials provided are properly verified in the message handler:

```
//capture the response object and add WWW-Authenticate header if the request was marked as unauthor
return base.SendAsync(request, cancellationToken)
    .ContinueWith(task =>
                {
                    HttpResponseMessage response = task.Result;
        ⊞ ● response {StatusCode: 200, ReasonPhrase: 'OK', Version: 1.1, Content: System.Net.Http.ObjectContent`1[[
                    && !response.Headers.Contains("WWW-Authentication"))
                    {
                        response.Headers.Add("WWW-Authentication", "Basic");
                    }
```

Now let's proceed to the next section, where the authentication data will be used for access-control of the action methods.

Authorization

All the controller action methods that we have created so far are unsecured, which means that they can be accessed by users who are not authenticated. Now that we have seen how we can authenticate requests, let's see how to use that information to authorize access to certain controllers or action methods.

The authorization process in Web API happens later in the pipeline after authentication, and before the controller actions are executed. This helps in providing access control depending on the authenticated user.

For authorization, Web API uses **authorization filters**, which respond with an error if the request is not authenticated and prevents the execution of protected action methods.

Using AuthorizeAttribute

Web API provides an authorization filter called AuthorizeAttribute. This attribute verifies the request's IPrincipal, checks its Identity.IsAuthenticated property, and returns a **401 Unauthorized** HTTP status if the value is false and the requested action method will not be executed.

The AuthorizeAttribute property can be applied in three levels:

- Global
- Controller
- Action levels

Global level

Global implementation is achieved by adding AuthorizeAttribute to the global filters list. See the following code snippet for example:

```
public static void Register(HttpConfiguration config)
{
    config.Filters.Add(new AuthorizeAttribute());
}
```

Once this code is added, only authenticated requests are allowed to invoke action methods in the Web API service.

Controller level

Decorating a controller with the [Authorize] attribute will prevent all action methods in the controller from being accessed by unauthorized users.

Let's create a new controller called AccountController and add an action method called RemoveUser to remove a user, and then decorate the controller with the [Authorize] attribute:

```
[Authorize]
    public class AccountController : ApiController
    {
        // GET api/account
        [HttpPost]
        public bool RemoveUser(int id)
        {
```

```
                //custom code to remove user
                return true;
            }
        }
```

Now let's try to invoke the `RemoveUser` action method without sending proper credentials and let's see what happens:

1. Open up Advanced Rest Client.

2. Select the request type as POST.

3. Hit the following URL:

   `http://localhost/movietickets.webapi/api/account/Removeuser/345`

   This action will display something like the following in the browser:

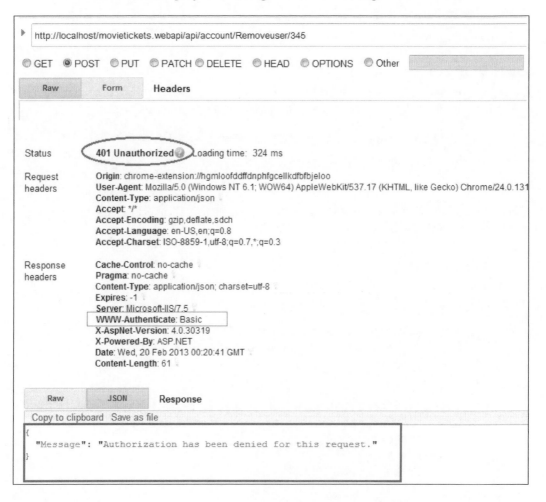

As you can see, Web API responded with a **401 Unauthorized** status code with the **WWW-Authenticate** header and this message:

```
"Message": "Authorization has been denied for this request."
```

If you got a pop up asking for credentials, just hit **Cancel**.

When proper credentials are sent for this request (that is, by adding the `Authorization: Basic dXN1cm5hbWU6cGFzc3dvcmQ=` header to the request), you will see that the action is executed and `true` is returned.

Action level

If you want to have both the protected and unprotected actions in the same controller, individual actions can be decorated with the `Authorize` attribute so that they require authenticated requests to invoke them while their actions can be executed by anonymous requests:

```
public class AccountController : ApiController
    {
        // GET api/account
        [HttpPost]
        [Authorize] //protected
        public bool RemoveUser(int id){...}

//Unprotected action
        public bool Login(UserBO user){...}
    }
```

[AllowAnonymous] attribute

This attribute marks the controllers and actions so that `AuthorizeAttribute` is skipped during the authorization. If there is a large number of protected actions in a controller, and very few are unprotected, the controller can be decorated with `[Authorize]` and the unprotected actions can be decorated with the `[AllowAnonymous]` attribute.

So the code mentioned in action-level authorization can be written like this:

```
[Authorize]
 public class AccountController : ApiController
    {
        // GET api/account
        [HttpPost]
        public bool RemoveUser(int id){...}

        [AllowAnonymous]
        public bool Login(UserBO user){...}
    }
```

Role and user checks

It is possible to filter certain roles and users too so that they are only granted access to the action methods.

Role checks can be done in two ways:

- Using `User.IsInRole("Admin")` within the action method code. User is the current principal and is defined in the `ApiController` base class.
- Using `[Authorize(Roles = "Admin")]` on the controllers and actions.

> If there are multiple roles and you need to check whether the user is in any of the roles, use `[Authorize(Roles = "Admin, PowerUser")]`.

Similarly, users can also be filtered:

- Using `User.Identity.Name.Equals("Bob")` within the action method code
- Using `[Authorize(User = "Bob")]` on controllers and actions

Custom authorization attribute

In real-world applications, where complex logic is used to implement authorization (for example, you want to prevent a certain range of IP addresses from invoking some action methods), the built-in `AuthorizationAttribute` may not suffice and we may have to rely on creating our own custom authorization filter. This can be achieved in three ways:

- By extending `AuthorizeAttribute` asynchronously
- By extending `AuthorizationFilterAttribute` synchronously
- By implementing `IAuthorizationFilter` asynchronously

Let's see how to extend the `AuthorizeAttribute` attribute and create a custom authorization attribute:

```
public class AdminUsersOnlyAttribute : AuthorizeAttribute
{
    protected override bool IsAuthorized(HttpActionContext context)
    {
        var currentPrincipal = Thread.CurrentPrincipal;
        // custom logic to check whether user is admin or not
    }
```

```
protected override void HandleUnauthorizedRequest(
  HttpActionContext actionContext)
{
    // custom response for unauthorized request
}
}
```

Now controllers and action methods can be decorated with the [AdminUsersOnly] attribute to prevent non-admin users from accessing them.

In order to reduce the complexity of the book, we are leaving the extending of AuthorizationFilterAttribute and implementing IAuthorizationFilter as an exercise for you.

Summary

In this chapter, we learned the features of ASP.NET Web API, and how to create a new Web API service and configure it. We also had a look at how Web API implements routing, parameter binding, Content Negotiation, and security. For the sample Movie Tickets application, we created a working structure of service with all the features we learned in this chapter. In the next chapter, we will explore the elements of the Kendo UI Framework and integrate Web API with our Kendo UI Mobile app.

4
Integration Using Framework Elements

In this chapter, we will get introduced to some of the important Kendo Framework elements such as DataSource, Templates, MVVM and more. Later in this chapter, we will discuss and see how to integrate the Web API backend with the Kendo UI frontend by building the User Account screen of the Movie Tickets application. We will also discuss how to modularize our JavaScript code by implementing a Revealing Module Pattern and see how to CORS enable our Web API service.

We will cover the following topics in this chapter:

- DataSource
- Templates
- MVVM
- Integrating with the Movie Tickets app

The Kendo UI's Framework elements differentiate Kendo UI from all the other HTML5/JavaScript frameworks available in the market by providing powerful components, which facilitates a solid base for building both web and mobile applications. While most other frameworks just provide certain features such as UI widgets, routing, templating, and so on individually, thanks to the framework elements, Kendo UI provides "simply everything" to build end-to-end web and mobile applications.

All of the Kendo's core framework elements can be used in both web as well as mobile applications without any limitations.

DataSource

It's quite a challenging experience for programmers to develop screens with a lot of JavaScript data manipulations such as filtering, sorting, paging, grouping, aggregating, and so on. Development becomes more complicated when remote and local data sources are involved.

Kendo's solution to this problem is the **DataSource** framework element, which makes developers' lives easy by abstracting all these complexities by providing commands to do common operations and becoming the single interface for all kinds of external and local data sources. It supports CRUD operations (Create, Read, Update, and Destroy) as well as filtering, sorting, paging, grouping, and aggregation of data.

A simple `DataSource` object can be initialized as:

```
var kendoDS = new kendo.data.DataSource();
```

This code does nothing but initialize a `DataSource` object without any data. To make this object useful, we need to provide data to the object or tell the object where it can fetch the data from. Let's look at some of the options to feed the local and remote data to DataSource.

Local data source

Sometimes developers will have data available locally in the form of JavaScript objects, which they need to bind into one or more widgets so that the users can work on them. It's very much convenient to bind local data to the `DataSource` object as most common operations can be performed on the data without writing much custom code.

From this chapter onwards, you will see a lot of examples uploaded to `jsfiddle.net`. **jsFiddle** is an online JavaScript live-coding environment, which helps developers to execute JS/HTML/CSS code and see the results using their web browser. Once you open the sample code in jsFiddle, you can click on the fork button to create your own version of the code with the existing code as the base. If you are new to online JS IDEs, the jsFiddle tutorial available in the following link will be a good place to explore:

`http://doc.jsfiddle.net/tutorial.html`

Let's see how we can bind a local JavaScript array to a `DataSource` object:

```
var videoGames = [{
    name: "Need for Speed: Underground",
```

```
        year: 2004,
        copiesSold: "1.10 million"
    }, {
        name: "Halo: Combat Evolved",
        year: 2001,
        copiesSold: "5 million"
    }, {
        name: "Grand Theft Auto Double Pack",
        year: 2003,
        copiesSold: "1.70 million"
    }];
    var videoGamesDS = new kendo.data.DataSource({
        data: videoGames
    });
```

That was easy, just assign the local JavaScript object to the `data` property at the time of initialization.

Now, let's call the `total()` method which gives the number of items in the `DataSource` in an `alert()` method to see if our data is loaded properly as shown in this code snippet:

```
alert(videoGamesDS.total());
```

The alert will return `0`, because we have only initialized the `DataSource` and didn't fill the `DataSource` object with the data. To make the data available in the `DataSource` object, we need to call the `read()` method. The `read()` method reads the data inside the `DataSource` object from the provided source. After updating the code with `read()`, we can see that the alert will display **3**, confirming that all three items are available in DataSource:

```
videoGamesDS.read();
alert(videoGamesDS.total());
```

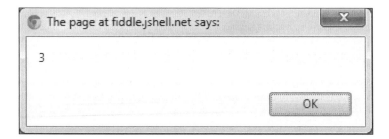

 Try it in jsFiddle:
http://jsfiddle.net/kendomobile/6FfWs/

Remote data source

It's a common scenario for mobile apps where data (typically JSON) needs to be fetched from a remote service using a provided URL. In this case, we need to add some more configuration while initializing DataSource. Here is how DataSource is initialized for a remote service that uses the JSON format:

```
var remoteDataSource = new kendo.data.DataSource({
    transport: {
        read: {
            // the remote url
            url: "http://yourdomain.com/jsonservice",

            // specify data format
            dataType: "json",

            // optional input parameters
            data: {
                inputParam: "inputParameterValue"
            }
        }
    },
    // describe result format
    schema: {
        // use data available in the "listOfItems" field
        data: "listOfItems"
    }
});
```

- transport: It specifies the settings for loading and saving data. Data can be loaded from a remote service, local file, or in-memory data.

- read: The settings for reading data are specified as:
  - url: It's the URL of the remote data / local file
  - dataType: It's the data format used for communication
  - data: It's the input parameter to remote service

- schema: It defines a structural organization of the received raw data. In the code earlier, we are specifying that the field listOfItems contains the data items. We can define data fields for aggregates, errors, total, groups, and parse too in the schema configuration.

`DataSource` is a very powerful object in the Kendo UI Framework and we just had an introduction to it. A complete discussion of `DataSource` is outside the scope of this book and therefore we would highly encourage you to explore DataSource further using Kendo documentation that's available in the following URLs:

- `http://goo.gl/psi3E`
- `http://goo.gl/iMVmD`

Templates

Templates are a simple and convenient way to build complex UI structures, typically with repeated blocks, which represent your view models. Kendo UI provides a powerful templating engine in the core framework, which is optimized for high performance. It has simplified syntax to make it easier to use with only the knowledge of JavaScript.

The templating syntax of Kendo UI (called hash templates) uses the # symbol to identify areas in a template where the data is to be inserted. They can be used in the following three ways:

1. `#= lastName #`: This renders the value stored in the variable `lastName`.

2. `#: address #`: This renders the value with its HTML encoding. This is useful to prevent rendering issues with user-input fields. For example, if the value of the address is provided as:

   ```
   <div> 123, streetname, state </div>
   ```

   Then the rendered HTML on the screen will show:

   `<div> 123, streetname, state </div>`

3. `#for(... ){# ... #}#`: This executes JavaScript code in the template so that rendering happens depending on certain conditions, such as loops. The template `#for(i=0;i<3; i++){#value of i: #=i# <br/> #}#` will render the following:

   ```
   value of i: 0
   value of i: 1
   value of i: 2
   ```

Rendering templates

The `kendo.template()` method is used for templating in the Kendo UI Framework. It returns the compiled template as a JavaScript function that renders the HTML using the data provided to it. Usage is pretty simple; provide the template as input to `kendo.template()` and call the compiled function with input data to generate the HTML.

Inline templates

Templates can be defined either as JavaScript strings (inline) or as HTML `<script>` blocks (external). Simple templates are the right candidates to be defined inline and more complicated templates with HTML blocks and JS expressions are better defined externally.

Here is a simple example for an inline template:

```
<div id="renderHere"> </div>
```

```
var kendoTemplate = kendo.template("This awesome HTML5 framework is
called : #= frameworkName # !");
var localData = { frameworkName: "Kendo UI" };
$("#renderHere").html(kendoTemplate(localData));
```

The output of the previous code will show **This awesome HTML5 framework is called : Kendo UI!**

 If a # needs to be in the templates, it needs to escape using backslash (\). In inline templates, since the template is a JavaScript string, \\ must be used before the #.

In the previous example, if we want to display output as **The #1 HTML5 framework is Kendo UI!**, then we need to change the template as:

```
var kendoTemplate = kendo.template("The \\#1 HTML5 framework is
#= frameworkName # !");
```

 Try it in jsFiddle:
http://jsfiddle.net/kendomobile/LHfbg/

External templates

External templates are defined in HTML files within `<script>` blocks with type `text/x-kendo-template` as shown:

```
<script id="kendoExternalTemplate" type="text/x-kendo-template" >
      <!--Template content goes here-->
   </script>
```

Since they are defined outside of the code, it's easy to code and maintain. External templates should have an ID as it is the handle used to select the template contents. Let's now see a little more complex external template example.

In this example, we will use an array of data that contains the mobile OS name and version number. If the version is outdated, a message will be displayed asking for the user to upgrade the OS.

In the template, we are using the escape character to display # in the output window and the template is rendered using the `kendo.render(template, data)` method.

 The `kendo.render()` method is used to render an array of JS objects.

```
<!-- div in which template will be rendered -->
<div id="renderHere"></div>

<!-- External Template definition -->
<script id="kendoExternalTemplate" type="text/x-kendo-template">
    #    switch (data.osName) {
        case "iOS":
            if (data.version < 6.1) {
                # <div> Your iOS version \# #= data.version# needs
                to be updated </div>
        #}
        break;
        case "Android":
        if(data.version < 3 ){#
        <div> Your Android version \# #=data.version# needs to
        be updated </div > #
            }
            break;
    }#
</script>
```

```
<script>
var localData = [{
            osName: "iOS",
            version: 6.1
        }, {
            osName: "Android",
            version: 2.3
        }, {
            osName: "iOS",
            version: 5.1
        }, {
            osName: "Android",
            version: 4.2
        }
    ];
    var kendoTemplate = kendo.template($("#kendoExternalTemplate").
html());
    $("#renderHere").html(kendo.render(kendoTemplate, localData));
</script>
```

The output of this code is:

Your Android version # 2.3 needs to be updated

Your iOS version # 5.1 needs to be updated

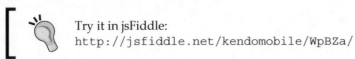

Try it in jsFiddle:
http://jsfiddle.net/kendomobile/WpBZa/

MVVM

Another important reason to choose Kendo UI over other HTML5 frameworks is the built-in support for MVVM. Most of the competing frameworks need developers to use third-party JS frameworks such as **KnockoutJS** to implement the MVVM pattern. Ever since MVVM was provided as part of the framework, developers don't have to worry about integration issues and support.

MVVM design pattern

Model-View-ViewModel (**MVVM**) is an architectural design pattern evolved from Microsoft, which attempts to separate the data model from the user interface. All the three members have their own responsibilities which clearly distinguish them from each other:

- **Model:** It contains the data points or application data (usually returned by the application logic layer).

- **View**: It is the user interface layer where the data is presented to the user.

- **ViewModel**: It is also known as the View's Model which acts as an intermediary between the view and the model. It creates an abstraction layer of the view as a model with data, commands, and abstractions, often aggregating multiple models.

Since ViewModel is a reflection of the view with its data, changes made on the view can automatically be reflected on the ViewModel and vice versa, which is achieved through **data bindings**. So by using MVVM, the amount of JavaScript code written, to update UI from data source and data source from UI is reduced dramatically as these two processes happen automatically. The developer needs to do nothing but define the binding between ViewModel and the UI elements.

 See this link for an excellent article by Addy Osmani, which discusses MVVM for JavaScript developers in detail:

`http://goo.gl/PahnJY`

Getting started with Kendo MVVM

The process of getting started with Kendo MVVM is very simple. Here is what we have to do:

- Create an observable ViewModel from JavaScript data using `kendo.observable()`

- Bind the methods and properties in the ViewModel to HTML elements in the UI using `kendo.bind()`

Now when the data changes the ViewModel, the changes are reflected in the UI, and when the UI data is changed by user interaction or by any arbitrary code, the ViewModel is also automatically updated with the change. Let's see how to do this using a simple example while we move into complex examples later:

HTML

```
<div id="mainView" >
    <input type="text" id="item" data-bind="value: item" />
    <input type="text" id="quantity" data-bind="value: quantity" />
    <br/>
     <label data-bind="text: description"> </label>
</div>
```

JavaScript

```
<script>
var observableViewModel = kendo.observable({
    item: "gold",
    quantity: "10 grams",
    description: function(){
     return     "You bought " + this.get("quantity") + " of "
     + this.get("item") ;
     }
});
//bind the view model
kendo.bind($("#mainView"),observableViewModel);
</script>
```

We created an observable ViewModel with two properties called `item` and `quantity` and a function. The properties are then bound to two textboxes and a **dependent method** called `description`, which uses the values of the properties in real time to create a description of the purchase that is bound to a label.

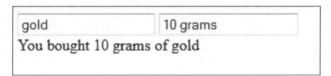

When the values in the textboxes are changed, it's automatically reflected in the description.

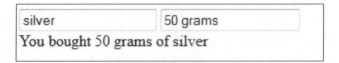

In the `description` function, we have used `this.get()` to read the values of `quantity` and `item`. The `get()` method is used to get the values of the properties in `observableViewModel` object. Similarly, a `set` method is used to set the values.

If we don't use the `get` method, the dependency on the binding won't be detected and the updated values won't be reflected when it is read. In the same way, we need to use a `set` method when the ViewModel's individual properties are modified so that the dependency on the binding is intact.

 Try it in jsFiddle:
`http://jsfiddle.net/kendomobile/wY74g/`

Bindings

An MVVM binding binds an HTML element/widget to a property or a method in the ViewModel. In the previous example we explored `text` and `value` bindings:

```
<input type="text" id="item" data-bind="value: item"/>
<input type="text" id="quantity" data-bind="value: quantity"/>
 <label data-bind="text: description"> </label>
```

Kendo MVVM supports several other bindings also so as to cover common scenarios where data binding is often used. Here is the full list of MVVM bindings:

Binding	Description
Attr	DOM element attributes are bound to ViewModel fields or methods.
	For example, `<a id="anchor" data-bind="attr: { href: url }"> Link </a>`
Checked	It checks/unchecks checkable DOM elements and widgets based on the values from the ViewModel.
	For example, `<input type="checkbox" data-bind="checked: IsSelected" />`
Click	In this binding, a method of the ViewModel is attached to the click DOM event of the bound element.
	For example, `<a data-role="button"` `data-bind="click:updateUserDetails"> Update </a>`
Custom	A custom binding can be registered by extending the `kendo.data.Binder` object. If you are interested in more information, complete documentation can be found in `http://goo.gl/tFksg`

Binding	Description
Disabled	The bound DOM element (applicable only to `input`, `select`, and `textarea`) will be made disabled depending on the ViewModel's property value or method.
	For example `<input type="text" data-bind="disabled: isDisabled" />`
Enabled	The bound DOM element (applicable only to `input`, `select`, and `textarea`) will be made enabled depending on the ViewModel's property value or method.
	For example, `<input type="text" data-bind="disabled: isEnabled" />`
Events	The ViewModel methods are bound to DOM events.
	For example, `<input type="text" data-bind="value:randomText, events:{focus: onFocus}" />`
Html	The HTML content (`innerHTML`) of the target DOM element is bound to the ViewModel's value.
	For example, `<div data-bind="html:htmlText">  </div>`
Invisible	A bound DOM element or widget is hidden or shown depending on the ViewModel's value.
	For example, `<input type="text" data-bind="invisible: isInvisible" />`
Visible	A bound DOM element or widget is shown or hidden depending on the ViewModel's value.
	For example, `<input type="text" data-bind="visible: isVisible" />`
Source	The target element's HTML content is set by rendering a Kendo template specified as the `data-template` attribute of the element with a ViewModel's value.
	For example, `<ul data-role="listview" data-style="inset" id="usracc-bkng-hstry-list" data-template="usracc-booking-history-tmpl" data-bind="source: userBookingHistory"></ul>`
Style	This way of binding sets the `style` attribute of a target DOM element.
	For example, `<span data-bind="style:{color:movieColor, fontSize:movieFontSize }, text: movieName"></span>`

Binding	Description
Text	The text content of a target DOM element is bound to a ViewModel's value.
	For example, `<label data-bind="text: description"></label>`
Value	Value binding supports HTML elements input, `textarea` and `select`. All the widgets having a value attribute are also supported.
	For example, `<input type="text" id="item" data-bind="value: item" />`

The Kendo team has provided an excellent explanation of all the bindings in detail at the following link:

`http://goo.gl/sMrfp`

MVVM in mobile

Kendo provides excellent support for MVVM in the mobile framework too. All the widgets in a mobile view can be bound to a ViewModel using the `model` configuration option. When the mobile view is initialized, `kendo.bind()` is invoked on all its child elements using the provided ViewModel in the `model` configuration. Since Kendo provides excellent touch support for its Web and DataViz widgets, they can be added to mobile applications too. In such scenarios, the mobile view will bind Mobile, Web, and DataViz widgets in the same order.

For declarative binding to work, as explained before in this section, the model object must be available in the **global scope** of the application.

Now let's take a look at a complex example in mobile view, which uses templates and MVVM.

The following code will expect a movie name as an input in a textbox, and append it to a list of movies. By clicking on the **X** button, movies can be removed from the list.

HTML

```html
<div data-role="view" style="margin: 10 0 0 4" data-model="viewModel">
    Movie:
    <input type="text" data-bind="value: movie" />
    <a data-bind="click: addMovie" data-role="button"
    id="btnAdd">Add</a>
    <div style="margin-top: 10px">
        Watched movies list:
        <ul data-template="movie-list-template"
        data-bind="source: movieList">
        </ul>
    </div>
</div>
<!--Kendo template -->
<script id="movie-list-template" type="text/x-kendo-template">
<li>
    Movie: <span data-bind="style:{color:movieColor,
    fontSize:movieFontSize },
    text: movieName"></span> |
    Added: <span data-bind="text: addedDate,
                style:{color:addedDateColor}"></span>
    <a data-bind="click: removeMovie"
 data-role="button"  id="btnRemove" >X</a>
</li>
</script>
```

JavaScript

```javascript
<script>
    var app = new kendo.mobile.Application(document.body);
    var viewModel = {
        movie: '',
        movieList: [],
        addMovie: function (e) {

//when addMovie function is called, add the movie
// property which is bound to the movie text box to
//movieList array along with styles and added date

            if (this.movie != '') {
                this.get("movieList").push(
        { movieName: this.get("movie"),
```

```
                            movieColor: "green",
                            movieFontSize: "16px",
                            addedDate:
                            new Date().toLocaleDateString(),
                            addedDateColor: "navy"
                        });
                    }

                    //clear the value in the text box.
                    this.set("movie", '');
                },

                removeMovie: function (e) {
                    alert('Remove: ' + e.data.movieName);

                    //Remove the movie name from the movieList array.
                    this.set("movieList",
        jQuery.grep(this.movieList,
          function (item, i) {
                        return (item.movieName != e.data.movieName);
                    }));
                }
            }
        </script>
```

The viewModel object is configured as the model to the mobile view using the data-model attribute. The **Add** button's click event, is bound to the addMovie function and the text entered in the textbox is added to the movieList array. Using Kendo UI **MVVM source binding**, the movieList array is bound to the template with the ID: movie-list-template. So the list of movies is automatically updated when the **Add** button is clicked. The removeMovie function is bound to the **X** button inside the template, which removes the selected movie from the list.

Inside the template, the style applied to movie names and dates added are bound using Kendo **MVVM Style binding**. The properties, which are bound using this binding, are movieColor, movieFontSize, and addedDateColor of the movieList object.

 Try it in jsFiddle:
http://jsfiddle.net/kendomobile/2PGkJ/

Integrating with the Movie Tickets app

As we have now covered some of the important elements of the Kendo UI Framework, let's put it all together and see how this works in a real-life application —Movie Tickets, by creating the User Account screen. We will also integrate our Web API service with the UI and work with some real data.

The User Account screen

Through the User Account screen, a registered user can log in to the application. Once the user is logged in, he/she can view and update his/her details. In this screen, the user is shown his/her ticket booking history too. After the user logs in, a **Log Off** button is displayed on the navigation bar.

Backend – setting up a Web API service

As the first step, let's configure the Web API service with the `Account` controller, a `GET` and a `POST` method, and set up some hardcoded data in the repository class.

> The service methods created in this chapter are accessible online using this URL:
>
> `http://api.kendomobilebook.com/api/Account/`

1. Create two classes named `UserBO.cs` and `TicketsBO.cs` inside the `BusinessObjects\BLL` folder. The objects of these classes will contain the User and Ticket details:

```
namespace MovieTickets.WebAPI.BLL
{
    public class TicketBO
    {
        public int TicketId { get; set; }
        public string TheaterName { get; set; }
        public string MovieName { get; set; }
        public  string Screen { get; set; }
        public int NoOfPersons { get; set; }
        public string ShowDate { get; set; }
        public string ShowTime { get; set; }
    }
}
```

```
namespace MovieTickets.WebAPI.BLL
{
    public class UserBO
    {
        public string FirstName { get; set; }
        public string LastName { get; set; }
        public string UserName { get; set; }
        public string Password { get; set; }
        public string EmailId { get; set; }
        public string Address { get; set; }
        public bool SubscribedForNewsLetter { get; set; }
        public List<TicketBO> BookingHistory { get; set; }
    }
}
```

2. In the `MovieRepository.cs` class, create a method called `GetUserDetails`. This method contains the hardcoded data of all the users with their ticket-booking history as shown in the following:

```
//This method will send user details back to the app
public static UserBO GetUserDetails(string userName)
{
    //2 users are created by default
    var usersList = new List<UserBO>{
        new UserBO(){
            Address = "123 North Field Pkwy,
                    Buffalo Grove, Illinois",
            EmailId = "alison.massey@email.com",
            FirstName = "Alison",
            LastName = "Massey",
            UserName = "username1",
            SubscribedForNewsLetter = true,
            BookingHistory = new List<TicketBO>{
                new TicketBO(){
                TicketId = new Random().Next(10000),
                TheaterName = "AMC, South
                                Barrington, IL",
                MovieName = "The Call",
                Screen = "12",
                NoOfPersons = 5,
                ShowDate = "15-Aug-2013",
                ShowTime = "4:30 PM"
                },
                new TicketBO(){
                TicketId = new Random().Next(10000),
```

```
                        TheaterName = "Regal Cinemas,
                            Lincolnshire, IL",
                    MovieName = "Argo",
                    Screen = "7",
                    NoOfPersons = 2,
                    ShowDate = "25-Aug-2013",
                    ShowTime = "7:00 PM"
                    }

            },
        },

    new UserBO(){
            Address = "20627 Mauve Orchid Way,Dallas, TX ",
            EmailId = "patrick.dcoster@email.com",
            FirstName = "Patrick",
            LastName = "DCoster",
            UserName = "username",
            SubscribedForNewsLetter = false,
            BookingHistory = new List<TicketBO>{
                    new TicketBO(){
                    TicketId = new Random().Next(10000),
                    TheaterName = "AMC NorthPark, North
                                    Central Expressway,
                                    Dallas, TX",
                    MovieName = "Evil Dead",
                    Screen = "19",
                    NoOfPersons = 6,
                    ShowDate = "13-July-2013",
                    ShowTime = "4:30 PM"
                    },
                    new TicketBO(){
                    TicketId = new Random().Next(10000),
                    TheaterName = "AmStar 14, Technology
                                    Boulevard, Dallas, TX",
                    MovieName = "The Host",
                    Screen = "21",
                    NoOfPersons = 1,
                    ShowDate = "21-Sept-2013",
                    ShowTime = "5:00 PM"
                    }
            },
        }
    };
```

```
        return usersList.FirstOrDefault(x => x.UserName.
Equals(userName));
    }
```

3. In the `MovieTicketsBLL` class, which we created in *Chapter 3*, *Service Layer with ASP.NET Web API*, create a method called `GetLoggedInUserDetails` that will retrieve a user's details and ticket history from the `GetUserDetails` method created in the earlier step:

```
public static UserBO GetLoggedInUserDetails(string userName)
{
return MovieRepository.GetUserDetails(userName);
}
```

4. Now in the `AccountController` (create a Web API controller called `AccountController` if you haven't created one already), create two methods called `Get` and `Post` as shown in the following code. The `Get` method will return details of the user and the `Post` method updates the user details (again, we don't really update the details in a persistent way as we are using hardcoded data; we are demonstrating how to do a POST and retrieve the values in the controller.):

```
[Authorize]
public UserBO Get()
{
    /* The user will be authenticated and
    Thread.CurrentPrincipal is set in the
    ValidateCredentials method of AuthMessagehandler class
    before the control reaches this action method */

    MovieTicketsPrincipal currentPrincipal =
    Thread.CurrentPrincipal as MovieTicketsPrincipal;

    return MovieTicketsBLL.GetLoggedInUserDetails(
        currentPrincipal.UserName);
}

[Authorize]
public bool Post(UserBO updatedUserDetails)
{
    //Code to update user details in the DB.
    //Since we are using hard coded values for the
    //demo, no save operation is done here.

    return true;
}
```

Frontend – architecture

Now that our Web API is ready with two action methods for the User Account screen, it's time to focus on the frontend UI of our mobile view. To start with, let's create the frontend architecture using jQuery/JavaScript to create ViewModels, data access methods, and some utility methods. We will treat each of these as separate modules by using JavaScript closures and implementing encapsulation. We will create each module in its own file and allow only certain functions and variables publicly accessible through the module objects.

Revealing Module Pattern

The design pattern we are following in our sample application for the JavaScript code is called **Revealing Module Pattern (RMP)**. The concept is very simple; we are introducing `private` and `public` encapsulation in JavaScript using closures. Only the methods and variables that are specifically returned are available publicly and we can provide references to privately declared methods and variables inside the public methods. Let's see an example of a module written in RMP:

```javascript
var applicationModule = (function() {

    //private variable. Existence limited within
    //this closure
    var privateVariable = 10;

    var privateFunction = function() {
        //Not accessible publicly
    };

 //accessibly publicly as
//applicationModule.publiclyReturnPrivateVar
    var publicFunction = function() {

        return privateVariable;

    };

    return {

        publiclyReturnPrivateVar: publicFunction

    };

})();

//prints value of privateVariable
console.log(applicationModule.publiclyReturnPrivateVar());
```

Try it in jsFiddle:
http://jsfiddle.net/kendomobile/gejfm/

We created a module called `applicationModule` containing a `private` variable by the name `privateVariable`, a `private` function by the name `privateFunction`, and a `public` function called `publicFunction`. The method `publicFunction` is accessible to the outside world only using `applicationModule.publiclyReturnPrivateVar`. The objects, `privateVariable` and `privateFunction`, are not at all accessible outside of the closure. The final parenthesis causes the function to be invoked.

Thus making use of closures in JavaScript, we implemented encapsulation available in other conventional object-oriented languages. Therefore, we can implement `Get` and `Set` properties like in C# by creating a `private` object and by creating `public` methods for "getting" and "setting" the values of the `private` object.

Advantages

By implementing the Revealing Module Pattern, we can build scalable and complex applications using JavaScript. Some of the advantages of this pattern are:

- The ability to hide methods and properties outside of the module
- It's easier to show call stacks in debugger
- It increases readability by clearly distinguishing `public` objects inside the `return` statement

If you want to explore more, we recommend you to read about Module Pattern and Revealing Module Pattern in Addy Osmani's book *Learning JavaScript Design Patterns* available in the following link:

http://goo.gl/y7wsV

Designing your JavaScript modules is really important in big projects as the team becomes bigger and bigger as there are more chances of programmers abusing freely available JavaScript objects in the global scope.

Namespacing

Many programming languages implement **namespacing** to avoid collisions with other objects or variables in the global namespace. It also helps in grouping an application's code into multiple blocks. Namespacing is important in applications written in JavaScript because of a high risk of conflicts that could happen in the global scope. Even though JavaScript does not have namespaces built in, we can still use JavaScript objects to provide namespace support.

In our Movie Tickets application we are defining a global object as our namespace as shown:

```
var MovieTickets = MovieTickets || {};
```

The `MovieTickets` object is defined inside the `<head> </head>` section before any other custom JS files are referenced so that this is the first object in our application to be initialized. Now we will create other modules as properties of this object so there won't be any collision with names defined by other third-party JS libraries we may use.

For example, our `configuration` module and `common` module will be available as:

```
MovieTickets.configuration
MovieTickets.common
```

Configuration

Typically in every software project, there will be a module to handle all the configuration data. For this purpose, in our project, let's create a file called `configuration.js` in the `scripts` folder. This module stores all the configurable data such as the Web API service's base and relative controller URLs:

```
MovieTickets.configuration = (function () {
    var serviceUrl = "http://localhost/movietickets.webapi/api/";
    return {
        serviceUrl: serviceUrl,
        accountUrl: serviceUrl + "Account/"
    }
})();
```

Now service and account controller URLs are available in the application in the following manner:

```
MovieTickets.configuration.serviceUrl MovieTickets.configuration.
accountUrl
```

If you are using a different URL to host your Web API service, replace the value of the `private` variable `serviceUrl` with your URL.

Data access

Now we need to create a re-usable data access module, which will be used to connect to the Web API and get the data for each view. For this create a file called data-access.js in the scripts folder and add the following code in it:

```javascript
MovieTickets.dataAccess = (function() {

    //options input parameter will have all the data needed
    //to perform the ajax call
    function callService(options) {

        $.ajax({
            url: options.url,
            type: options.requestType,
            data: options.data,
            dataType: options.dataType,

            //Add HTTP headers if configured
            beforeSend: function (xhr) {
                if (typeof options.httpHeader !== 'undefined'
                    && typeof options.headerValue !== 'undefined')
                    xhr.setRequestHeader(options.httpHeader,
                        options.headerValue);
            },
            //on successful ajax call back
            success: function (resultData, status, xhr) {
                var result = {
                    data: resultData,
                    success: true
                };
                options.callBack(result);
            },
            //Callback function in case of an error
            error: function (xhr, status, errorThrown) {

                switch (xhr.status) {

                    case '401':
                        alert('401 Unauthorized access detected.
                            Please check the credentials
                        you entered.' + errorThrown);
                        break;
                    case '500':
                        alert('500 Internal Server Error.
```

```
                              Please check the service code.'
                                 + errorThrown);
                        break;
                    default:
                        alert('Unexpected error: ' + errorThrown);
                        break;
                }
                var result = { success: false };
                options.callBack(result);
            }
        });
    }

    return {
        callService: callService
    }
})();
```

This module exposes a method called `MovieTickets.dataAccess.callService()`, which calls a service using the URL provided and perform the actions configured in the `options` object:

- `options.url`: The URL to be invoked
- `options.requestType`: Type of request, for example GET, POST, PUT, DELETE and so on
- `options.data`: Data to be sent to the service
- `options.dataType`: Type of data expected back from the server, for example JSON/XML and so on
- `options.httpHeader`: HTTP header that needs to be added along with the request
- `options.headerValue`: Value of the added HTTP header
- `options.callBack`: Function to be invoked once the response is received

Using these configurations from the options object, a jQuery Ajax call is made to the service and the `callback` function is invoked. If the request succeeded, the data returned from the server is returned along with the `callback` function containing a success flag value `true` ({ `success: true` }), and if an error is encountered, the `callback` function is called with an error flag ({ `success: false` }).

In the `error` function of jQuery, we display friendly error messages depending on the common error codes such as **500** (Internal server error), **401**(Unauthorized access), and more.

Initialization

Let's reorganize the application's initialization code from *Chapter 2, Building Your First Mobile Application,* so as to create a formal structure for the project. In order to do this, let's create a file called `movie-tickets.js` in the `scripts` folder and move the application initialization code along with some more code to this file. The module called `MovieTickets.main` will act as the main entry point of the application:

```
MovieTickets.main = (function () {
    var application;

    function getApplication() {
        return application;
    }

    function initializeApp() {

        //initialize app
        application = new kendo.mobile.Application(document.body,
         {
             transition: 'slide',
             loading: "<h3>Loading...</h3>"

         });

        //Display loading image on every ajax call
        $(document).ajaxStart(function () {

            //application.showLoading calls the showLoading()
            //method of the pane object inside the application.
            //During the application's initial view's init
            //method this pane object may not be initialized
            //and so application.showLoading() may throw error.
            //To prevent this we need to do a check for existence
            //application.pane before calling
            //application.showLoading();
            if (application.pane) {
                application.showLoading();
            }
        });

        //Hide ajax loading image on after ajax call
        $(document).ajaxStop(function () {

            if (application.pane) {
```

```
                application.hideLoading();
            }
        });
    }

    return {
        initializeApp: initializeApp,
        getKendoApplication: getApplication
    }
})();
```

In this module, we are initializing the application using the `kendo.mobile.Application()` method, and setting up the initial view as the home page, the view transition effect as `slide`, and the Ajax loading text as `<h3>Loading...</h3>`. Once the Kendo UI Mobile app is initialized, we used the `$(document).ajaxStart` and `$(document).ajaxStop` events of jQuery to display and hide loading message whenever an Ajax call is fired from our application, thus preventing the need to explicitly show and hide loading messages in Ajax calls.

Common utility methods

Now, let's create the `MovieTickets.common` module in a file called `common.js` in the `scripts` folder, where utility methods invoked by multiple modules can be written. We will add three methods:

- `navigateToView(view)`: In this method, we are using the Kendo `application` object's `navigate()` method to navigate to a particular view programatically. The view can be local, remote, or external view.

- `showLogOffButton()`: This method, when invoked, displays the **Log Off** button on the navigation bar (the HTML code for this will be added later in the chapter).

- `hideLogOffButton()`: This method hides the **Log Off** button on the navigation bar.

```
MovieTickets.common = (function () {

    function navigateToView(view) {
        //Navigate to local/remote or external view
        MovieTickets.main.getKendoApplication().navigate(view);
    }
    function showLogOffButton() {
        //show log off button.
        $(".mt-main-layout-btn-logoff").show();
    }
```

```
function hideLogOffButton() {
    //hide log off button
    $(".mt-main-layout-btn-logoff").hide();
}

return {
    navigateToView: navigateToView,
    showLogOffButton: showLogOffButton,
    hideLogOffButton: hideLogOffButton
}

})();
```

 In the navigateToView function, we can even navigate to the previous view using #:back as an input parameter.

User Account ViewModel

Since now we have the base of our project set, we can create an observable ViewModel for the User Account screen, which will be bound to the view using the data-model attribute as described in the *MVVM* section. Let's create a file called user-account.js in the scripts folder and add the following code:

```
MovieTickets.userAccount = (function () {
    //ViewModel for User Account view
    var viewModel = kendo.observable({
        isUserLoggedIn: false,
        firstName: "",
        lastName: "",
        userName: "username", //hardcoded
        password: "password", //hardcoded
        userAddress: "",
        userEmailAddress: "",
        subscribedForNewsLetter: false,
        userBookingHistory: [],
        userLogin: function () {
            var loginOptions = {
                url: MovieTickets.configuration.accountUrl,
                requestType: "GET",
                dataType: "JSON",
                //for HTTP Basic authentication
                httpHeader: "Authorization",
```

```
            //btoa function will convert the text to
            //base 64 encoding
            headerValue: "Basic "
                + btoa(this.userName + ":" + this.password),
            callBack: this.fnLoginCallBack
        };
        MovieTickets.dataAccess.callService(loginOptions);

    },
    //method for user login
    fnLoginCallBack: function (result) {
        if (result.success === true) {
            viewModel.set("firstName", result.data.FirstName);
            viewModel.set("lastName", result.data.LastName);
            viewModel.set("userAddress", result.data.Address);
            viewModel.set("userEmailAddress",
                result.data.EmailId);
            viewModel.set("userBookingHistory",
                result.data.BookingHistory);
            viewModel.set("isUserLoggedIn", true);
            viewModel.set("subscribedForNewsLetter",
                result.data.SubscribedForNewsLetter);

            MovieTickets.common.showLogOffButton();


        } else {
            //any error handling code
        }
    },


    //method to update user details
    updateUserDetails: function () {
        var updateOptions = {
            url: MovieTickets.configuration.accountUrl,
            requestType: "POST",
            dataType: "JSON",
            data: {
                firstName: viewModel.get("firstName"),
                lastName: viewModel.get("lastName"),
                address: viewModel.get("userAddress"),
                emailId: viewModel.get("userEmailAddress"),
                subscribedForNewsLetter:
                    viewModel.get("subscribedForNewsLetter")
            },
```

```
                        //for HTTP Basic authentication
                        httpHeader: "Authorization",
                        //btoa function will convert the text to
                        //base 64 encoding
                        headerValue: "Basic " + btoa(this.userName + ":"
                            + this.password),
                        callBack: function () {
                            //if you are using PhoneGap to deploy
                            //as an app, you should use the
                            //notification api
                            alert('Details updated...');
                        }
                    };
                    MovieTickets.dataAccess.callService(updateOptions);
                },

                //method called when log off button is clicked
                logOff: function () {
                    console.log('inside logOff');
                    viewModel.set("firstName", "");
                    viewModel.set("lastName", "");
                    viewModel.set("userAddress", "");
                    viewModel.set("userEmailAddress", "");
                    viewModel.set("userBookingHistory", "");
                    viewModel.set("isUserLoggedIn", false);

                    //hide log off button
                    MovieTickets.common.hideLogOffButton();

                    //navigate to User Account screen.
                    MovieTickets.common.navigateToView("UserAccount.html");
                }
            });

        return {
            viewModel: viewModel
        }
    })();
```

In the previous ViewModel code, we created properties related to user details, such as first name, last name, and more. We also created properties for booking history of the user to be displayed on the **User Account** screen. The ViewModel, which is accessible with `mtUserAccount.viewModel`, will be bound to the view using the `data-model` attribute. We have added the following functions too to the ViewModel, which will be invoked from the User Account screen:

- `userLogin()`: This function is used to log in to the system by invoking the `AccountController`'s method's `Get` action method. Since `Get` method is a secured using the `[Authorize]` attribute, we send the username and password of the user (which will be available when the properties are bound to the respective fields) in the HTTP header for Basic authentication. To do Base64 encoding, we are using the `btoa()` function.

- `fnLoginCallBack()`: This function is invoked when the response is received from the service for the login Ajax call (`callback`). If the login call succeeds, the ViewModel properties are set using values from the service. The `isUserLoggedIn` property is also set to `true` to indicate that the user is logged in to the app. This property will determine whether to show the user login screen or the user details screen to the user, when the user navigates to the User Account screen. Then the `MovieTickets.common.showLogOffButton()` method is called to display the **Log Off** button in the navigation bar.

- `updateUserDetails()`: The updated values of the `firstName`, `lastName`, `address`, `emailId`, and `subscribedForNewsLetter` properties which are collected from the User Account screen are sent to the Web API for saving.

  For this purpose, we are invoking the `POST` method of the account controller with the user credentials encoded as Base64 values, which are sent as headers.

- `Logoff()`: This method is used to clear user details from the ViewModel and log the user off. It will also redirect the user to the **User Account** screen as users can log off from anywhere in the application. For this purpose, we are using the `navigateToView` function of the `MovieTickets.Common` module.

 Since we are using a stateless HTTP-based service, you don't have to inform the service about logging off, as the service does not keep track of server-side sessions.

HTML UI

You would have got bored by now; writing JavaScript code when you really want to get your hands on the real Kendo UI Mobile code. Let's do it right away and write some HTML code and bring some Kendo widgets, templates, and bindings.

Adding the User Account TabStrip button

Let's now open the index.html file, which we created in *Chapter 2, Building Your First Mobile Application*, and add one more button to the TabStrip widget in the layout footer for navigation to the **User Account** screen. We are using the user_profile.ico icon file provided along with the source code as the icon for the button. The modified TabStrip code is as follows:

```html
<div data-role="tabstrip">
    <a href="#mt-home-main-view">
        <img src="images/movies.ico"
            height="40" width="40" />
        <br />
        Movies
    </a>
    <a href="Trailers.html">
        <img src="images/trailers.ico" height="40" width="40" />
        <br />
        Trailers
    </a>
    <a href="UserAccount.html">
        <img src="images/user_profile.ico" />
        My Account
    </a>

    <a href="#mt-about-view" data-icon="about">
        <br />
        About
    </a>
</div>
```

Now in the index.html file, replace the initialization code from *Chapter 2, Building Your First Mobile Application*, with the new initialization code:

```html
<script>
  //Kendo Mobile is initialized in this method
  MovieTickets.main.initializeApp();
</script>
```

Now the home screen will now look like the following screenshot:

User Account view

When we added the new `TabStrip` button in the previous section, we have also linked the **My Account** button to `UserAccount.html`, and now we are going to create this view as a **remote view**. Create `UserAccount.html` in the root folder and create a view with two `div` values; one for the login section which is to be displayed if the user is not logged in, and the other section which will display the user details once the user is logged in. We will then bind the view to the User Account ViewModel using `data-model="movieTickets.userAccount.viewModel"`. The visibility of the login section is then bound to the `isUserLoggedIn` property of the ViewModel using Kendo MVVM **Invisible binding** (see the *Bindings* section). Similarly, the user details section is bound to the property `isUserLoggedIn` using Kendo MVVM **Visible binding** as we need to show this section when the user is logged in.

```
<div data-role="view" data-layout="mt-main-layout"
    data-title="Account"
    data-model="MovieTickets.userAccount.viewModel"
    id="mt-theaters-view">

    <!-- This section is bound by Kendo MVVM Invisible binding -->
    <div id="usracc-login-section"
        data-bind="invisible: isUserLoggedIn">
    </div>

    <div id="usracc-user-details"
        data-bind="visible: isUserLoggedIn">
    </div>
</div>
```

Login section

Let's now add some fields and binding in to both the sections. For the Login section, let's define a Kendo `ListView` widget and add fields for entering username and password along with a login button. The `ListView` widget is used here only to arrange the elements, and will be discussed in detail in the next chapter. Then we will bind them to the respective properties and functions in the ViewModel:

```
<ul data-role="listview" data-style="inset">
<li>
        <label>User Name:  </label>
            <input type="text" data-bind="value:userName"
 id="user-acc-username" />
        </li>
   <li>
            <label>Password:  </label>
    <input type="text" id="user-acc-password"
data-bind="value:password" />
</li>
</ul>

<div class="centerAlign">
<a data-role="button" id="user-acc-login-button"
    data-bind="click:userLogin">Login </a>
</div>
```

User details section

Next, let's add the UI elements for the user details section with text fields to display user details and a templated ListView to display the booking history of the user.

First we will create a Kendo template to display the booking history of the user, which will be added at the bottom of the file outside of the view:

```
<script type="text/x-kendo-template"
        id="usracc-booking-history-tmpl">

    Movie: <span class="valueText"> #=MovieName #</span>
        Tickets:   <span class="valueText"> #=NoOfPersons # </span>
    <br/>
    Theater:<span class="valueText"> #=TheaterName # </span>
    <br/>
    Screen: <span class="valueText">#=Screen # </span>
```

```
        Show Date: <span class="valueText"> #=ShowDate# </span>
<br/>
Time: <span class="valueText">#=ShowTime # </span>
```

```
</script>
```

This template will display the details of the tickets booked, for example, movie name, number of tickets, theater address, screen number, show date, and show time.

Now we will update the user details div with the ID usracc-user-details using the following code:

```
<div id="usracc-user-details"
    data-bind="visible: isUserLoggedIn ">
  <div>
      <ul data-role="listview">
          <li>First Name
              <input type="text" id="usracc-firstName"
                  data-bind="value: firstName" />
          </li>
          <li>Last Name
              <input type="text" id="usracc-lastName"
                  data-bind="value: lastName" />
          </li>
          <li>Address
              <input type="text" id="usracc-address"
                  data-bind="value: userAddress" />
          </li>
          <li>Email
              <input type="text" id="usracc-emailAddress"
                  data-bind="value: userEmailAddress" />
          </li>
          <li>Newsletter
              <span style="text-align: left">
                  <input type="checkbox" id="usracc-newsletter"
                      data-role="switch"
                      data-bind=
                      "checked: subscribedForNewsLetter" />
              </span>
```

```
            </li>
        </ul>
    </div>
    <br />
    <div class="centerAlign">

        <a data-role="button" id="usracc-btn-update"
            data-bind="click:updateUserDetails">Update </a>
    </div>

    <!--Booking History section-->
    <div>
        <h3>Booking History </h3>

        <!--Render template using MVVM Source binding -->
        <ul data-role="listview" data-style="inset"
            id="usracc-bkng-hstry-list"
            data-template="usracc-booking-history-tmpl"
            data-bind="source: userBookingHistory">
        </ul>
    </div>
</div>
```

In the previous code, we added fields to display the user details and an **Update** button. We have used the Kendo **Switch** widget to display the newsletter subscription status of the user and its checked state is bound to the subscribedForNewsLetter property. This widget will be discussed in detail in the next chapter. When we click on the **Update** button, it will call the updateUserDetails function in the ViewModel, which will in turn send the updated user details to the service as an HTTP POST request. After the user details section, the booking history template is rendered using a ListView widget with the data source as the userBookingHistory property in the ViewModel.

Once the user logs in to the app using the credentials such as username/password or username1/password1, the user details will be displayed on the view as shown in the following screenshot:

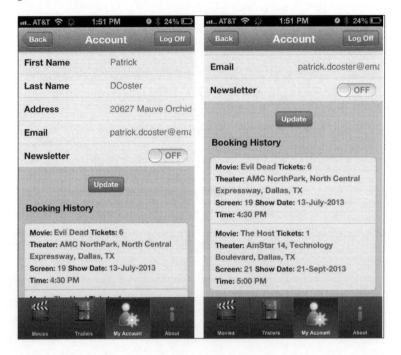

Fixing cross-domain access issues

If you host your Web API service in one domain and your mobile app is hosted in another domain (or if you are trying to access Web API hosted on your PC from the mobile website opened on your mobile phone), you may see that your Ajax calls to the Web API service are getting blocked. This happens because of the **same-origin policy** implemented in web browsers that restricts calls to the domain of the resource that makes the call. Using JSONP (JSON with padding) instead of JSON is a common solution, but it is considered as a hack and the recommended solution is to make your service **CORS (Cross-Origin Resource Sharing)** enabled. CORS is a **W3C** standard which allows web pages to make Ajax requests to a different domain. This standard relaxes the same-origin policy imposed by the browsers.

If you would like to explore CORS in detail, here is a good article from the Mozilla Developer Network available in the following link:

`http://goo.gl/TERopp`

We can make our Web API service globally CORS-enabled by adding the following configuration to the `<system.webServer>` `</system.webServer>` section of the `web.config` file of Web API:

```
<httpProtocol>
    <customHeaders>
    <add name="Access-Control-Allow-Origin"
        value="*"/>
    <add name="Access-Control-Allow-Headers"
        value="accept, authorization, origin, content-type"/>
    <add name="Access-Control-Allow-Methods"
        value="GET, POST, PUT, DELETE, OPTIONS"/>
    </customHeaders>
</httpProtocol>
```

The previous configuration allows requests from any origin with headers accept authorization, origin, and content-type for the method types GET, POST, PUT, DELETE, and OPTIONS.

After making this update to your `web.config`, you can host your Web API service at a domain at `xyz.com` and your web app hosted at another domain, for example, `abc.com` can access the Web API's service methods using Ajax!

At the time of writing this book, ASP.NET Web API is coming up with built-in CORS support which can be accessed through nightly builds. Yao Huang Lin has provided detailed instructions on how to use the new CORS support in the following URL:

`http://goo.gl/s61EJG`

Summary

In this chapter, we were introduced to some important Kendo UI Framework elements such as DataSource, Templates, and MVVM in detail. We also integrated the Web API service created in *Chapter 3, Service Layer with ASP.NET Web API*, with the Movie Tickets app and developed the User Account screen. We implemented HTTP Basic authentication in the Movie Tickets app to access some secured action methods. Using the Movie Tickets application, we also discussed how to structure a Kendo UI Mobile application using the Revealing Module Pattern. In the next chapter, we will dive deep into Kendo UI Mobile, learn about more Kendo UI Mobile widgets and do lots of hands-on exercises!

5
Exploring Mobile Widgets

Kendo UI Mobile allows programmers to develop mobile applications rapidly by providing a variety of theme-able widgets. These widgets are tailored for touch-based mobile devices and provide platform-specific rendering with a native a look and feel. In *Chapter 2, Building Your First Mobile Application*, we got introduced to the basic structure of Kendo Mobile application and some of the widgets. In this chapter, we will start exploring Kendo Mobile widgets from the basics and in detail with examples.

In this chapter we will cover:

- Kendo Mobile widgets basics
- Mobile UI widgets
- ListView
- Button
- ButtonGroup
- Switch
- Pane
- PopOver

Kendo Mobile widgets basics

All Kendo Mobile widgets inherit from the base class `kendo.mobile.ui.Widget`, which is inherited from the base class of all Kendo widgets (both Web and Mobile), `kendo.ui.Widget`. The complete inheritance chain of the mobile widget class is shown in the following figure:

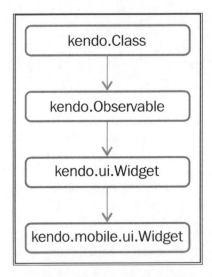

`kendo.Class` acts as the base class for most of the Kendo UI objects while the `kendo.Observable` object contains methods for events. `kendo.data.ObservableObject` which is the building block of Kendo MVVM, is inherited from `kendo.Observable`.

Mobile widget base methods

From the inheritance chain, all Kendo Mobile widgets inherit a set of common methods. A thorough understanding of these methods is required while building highly performing, complex mobile apps.

 Kendo UI Mobile supports only WebKit-based browsers and so it's important to use Chrome or Safari browsers to run the demo code on your desktop.

bind

The `bind()` method defined in the `kendo.Observable` class, attaches a handler to an event. Using this method we can attach custom methods to any mobile widget. The `bind()` method takes the following two input parameters:

- `eventName`: The name of the event
- `handler`: The function to be fired when the event is raised

The following example shows how to create a new mobile widget and attach a custom event to the widget:

```
//create a new mobile widget
var mobileWidget = new kendo.mobile.ui.Widget();

//attach a custom event
mobileWidget.bind("customEvent", function(e) {

  // mobileWidget object can be accessed inside this function as
    //'e.sender' and 'this'.
  console.log('customEvent fired');

});
```

The event data is available in the object `e`. The object which raised the event is accessible inside the function as `e.sender` or using the `this` keyword.

trigger

The `trigger()` method executes all event handlers attached to the fired event. This method has two input parameters:

- `eventName`: The name of the event to be triggered
- `eventData` (optional): The event-specific data to be passed into the event handler

Let's see how trigger works by modifying the code sample provided for bind:

```
//create a mobile widget
var mobileWidget = new kendo.mobile.ui.Widget();

//attach a custom event
mobileWidget.bind("customEvent", function(e) {

  // mobileWidget object can be accessed
  //inside this function as
```

```
            //'e.sender' and 'this' .
            console.log('customEvent fired');

            //read event specific data if it exists
            if(e.eventData !== undefined){
              console.log('customEvent fired with data: '
              + e.eventData);
            }
          });

          //trigger the event with some data
            mobileWidget.trigger("customEvent",
              { eventData:'Kendo UI is cool!' });
```

Here we are triggering the custom event which is attached using the `bind()` method and sending some data along. This data is read inside the event and written to the console.

When this code is run, we can see the following output in the console:

```
customEvent fired
customEvent fired with data: Kendo UI is cool!
```

Try it in jsFiddle:
http://jsfiddle.net/kendomobile/9grnR/

unbind

The `unbind()` method detaches a previously attached event handler from the widget. It takes the following input parameters:

- `eventName`: The name of the event to be detached. If an event name is not specified, all handlers of all events will be detached.

- `handler`: The handler function to be detached. If a function is not specified, all functions attached to the event will be detached.

The following code attaches an event to a widget and detaches it when the event is triggered:

```
          //create a mobile widget
          var mobileWidget = new kendo.mobile.ui.Widget();

          //attach a custom event
          mobileWidget.bind("customEvent", function(e) {
```

```
    console.log('customEvent fired');

    this.unbind("customEvent");

});

//trigger the event first time
mobileWidget.trigger("customEvent");

//trigger the event second time
mobileWidget.trigger("customEvent");
```

Output:

```
customEvent fired
```

As seen from the output, even though we trigger the event twice, only on the first time is the event handler invoked.

one

The one() method is identical to the bind() method only with one exception; the handler is unbound after its first invocation. So the handler will be fired only once.

To see this method in action, let's add a count variable to the existing sample code and track the number of times the handler is invoked. For this we will bind the event handler with one() and then trigger the event twice as shown in the following code:

```
//create a mobile widget
var mobileWidget = new kendo.mobile.ui.Widget();
var count = 0;
//attach a custom event
mobileWidget.one("customEvent", function(e) {
    count++;
    console.log('customEvent fired. count: ' + count);

});

//trigger the event first time
mobileWidget.trigger("customEvent");

//trigger the event second time
mobileWidget.trigger("customEvent");
```

Output:

```
customEvent fired. count: 1
```

 Try it in jsFiddle:
http://jsfiddle.net/kendomobile/TnF3e/

If you replace the one() method with the bind() method, you can see that the handler will be invoked twice.

 All the methods discussed previously (bind(), trigger(), unbind(), and one()) are not limited to widgets only, but are also available on any Kendo object derived from kendo.Observable.

destroy

The destroy() method is inherited from the kendo.ui.Widget base object. The destroy() method kills all the event handler attachments and removes the widget object in the jquery.data() attribute so that the widget can be safely removed from the DOM without memory leaks. If there is a child widget available, the destroy() method of the child widget will also be invoked.

Let's see how the destroy() method works using the Kendo Mobile Button widget and using your browser's developer tools' console. Create an HTML file, add the following code along with Kendo UI Mobile file references in the file, and open it in your browser:

```
<div data-role="view" >
  <a class="button" data-role="button" id="btnHome"
    data-click="buttonClick">Home</a>
</div>
<script>
  var app = new kendo.mobile.Application(document.body);

  function buttonClick(e){

    console.log('Inside button click event handler...');
    $("#btnHome").data().kendoMobileButton.destroy();

  }
</script>
```

In this code block, we created a Kendo Button widget and on the click event, we are invoking the `destroy()` method of the button.

 Try it online: `http://kendomobilebook.com/chapter5/destroy.html`

Now open up your browser's developer tools' **Console** window, type `$("#btnHome").data()` and press *Enter*.

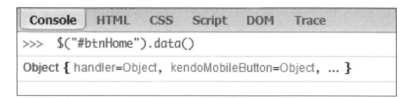

Now if you click on the **Object** link shown in the earlier screenshot, a detailed view of all properties can be seen:

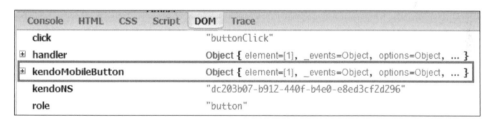

Now click on **kendoMobilebutton** once and then again in the **Console**, type `$("#btnHome").data()` and hit *Enter*. Now we can see that the **kendoMobileButton** object is removed from the object list:

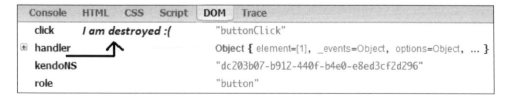

Even though the data object is gone, the button stays in the DOM without any data or events associated with it.

 If you want the button to be removed from the DOM too, you can call the jQuery.remove() method as shown:

```
$("#btnHome").remove();
```

view

The view() method is specific to mobile widgets and it returns the view object in which the widget is loaded.

In the previous example, we can assign an ID, mainView, to the view and then retrieve it in the button's click event using this.view().id as shown in the following code snippet:

```
<div data-role="view" id="mainView" >
  <a class="button" data-role="button" id="btnHome"
    data-click="buttonClick">Home</a>
</div>
<script>
  var app = new kendo.mobile.Application(document.body);

  function buttonClick(e){

    console.log("View id: " + this.view().id);
  }
</script>
```

Output:

```
View id: #mainView
```

 Try it in jsFiddle:
http://jsfiddle.net/kendomobile/xh4y7/

One scenario where the view() method is useful is on a widget's event. If another element/widget in the same view needs to be accessed, we can improve the performance of selecting the element by narrowing the search down using the current view's ID.

Suppose in the previous example we had an element in the same view with ID htmlElement, we can select the element using $(this.view().id).find("#htmlElement"), which will perform better than $("#htmlElement") if there are multiple views loaded in the DOM, as jQuery now needs to traverse less HTML elements.

Mobile UI widgets

Now let's get to the real deal and explore more Kendo UI Mobile widgets. We have used some of the widgets in *Chapter 2, Building Your First Mobile Application*, and in this chapter we will have a detailed look at more widgets.

These are the widgets provided by Kendo UI Mobile framework:

- ActionSheet
- Button
- ButtonGroup
- ListView
- ModalView
- NavBar
- PopOver
- Scroller
- ScrollView
- Switch
- TabStrip
- Touch
- Drawer (introduced in Q2 2013)

Now let's go over all the widgets which are new to you, study how they work, and towards the end of the chapter we will integrate these widgets into our Movie Ticket application.

 The intention of this chapter is to get you started with Kendo Mobile widgets with an explanation of some important properties and methods, their usage, and some important tips. We are not providing a complete documentation of all the properties and methods of all the widgets because in every quarterly release, properties and methods are added/deprecated and so Kendo's API reference documentation available at http://docs.kendoui.com/api/mobile is your best friend for a complete reference of the frameworks.

init and show events of the View widget

The Kendo UI Mobile View widget exposes two important events: `init` and `show`. Event handlers for these events can be wired using data attributes as shown:

```
<div data-role="view" data-init="onInitialize"
  data-show="onShow">
</div>

<script>
  var app = new kendo.mobile.Application(document.body);

  function onInitialize(e) {
    alert('view initialized');
  }

  function onShow(e) {
    alert('view shown');
  }

</script>
```

[Try it in jsFiddle:
http://jsfiddle.net/kendomobile/vWC39/   ]

The `init` event is fired first and only once, after the View and its child widgets are initialized. The `show` event is fired whenever the view becomes visible. The `init` event is designed to be used for actions which should be done only once during the life cycle of a view, for example, creating a widget programmatically using JavaScript code. This must not be done in the `show` event as the code will try to create the widget whenever the view becomes visible and causes unintended consequences.

The `show` event should be used for scenarios for actions which need to occur whenever the view is shown, for example, updating a widget with the latest data from the server whenever the view becomes visible.

The View widget exposes three more events:

- `beforeShow`: This event is fired just before the view becomes visible
- `afterShow`: This event is fired after the view becomes visible
- `hide`: This event is fired when the view becomes hidden

The ListView widget

In mobile devices, list is the most widely used user interface component. Lists are styled and modified in different ways so as to display a simple list of data having a complex structure. Kendo UI provides a very powerful List widget called the ListView which can be used to display flat, grouped, or custom template lists. Kendo will automatically convert any HTML list to a mobile optimized ListView widget when the `data-role="listview"` attribute is added to the list element:

```
<ul data-role="listview">
  <li>Olympus Has Fallen</li>
  <li>Jurassic Park 3D</li>
  <li>G.I. Joe: Retaliation</li>
</ul>
```

As with any other Kendo widget, ListView can be initialized programmatically too, using the jQuery plugin syntax as shown in the following code snippet:

```
<div data-role="view" data-init="initialize">
<ul id="myList"></ul>
</div>
<script>
function initialize(){

  $("#myList").kendoMobileListView({
      dataSource: ["Olympus Has Fallen",
    "Jurassic Park 3D",
    "G.I. Joe: Retaliation"]
      });
}

</script>
```

Try it in jsFiddle:
http://jsfiddle.net/kendomobile/72mKp/

Inset style

The code snippets we saw in the previous section will display a list which takes the entire width of the screen. If you are not happy with this experience and need your list to have a margin and rounded corners as in iOS devices, you can add the attribute data-style="inset" to the <ul> element. This setting is not applicable for Android or BlackBerry devices:

```
<ul data-role="listview" data-style="inset">
  <li>Olympus Has Fallen</li>
  <li>Jurassic Park 3D</li>
  <li>G.I. Joe: Retaliation</li>
</ul>
```

Try it in jsFiddle:
http://jsfiddle.net/kendomobile/g9GRs/

The previous figure shows the list with an inset style.

Links

If your list has anchor tags, Kendo ListView will automatically add right arrow indicators to the list, so that it is intuitive to the user that the items in the list are clickable for detailed view or navigation:

```
<ul data-role="listview" data-style="inset">
  <li><a>Olympus Has Fallen</a></li>
  <li><a>Jurassic Park 3D</a></li>
  <li><a>G.I. Joe: Retaliation</a></li>
</ul>
```

Detail buttons and icons

DetailButton widgets are button icons which are small in size and typically used to conserve space when multiple buttons are required in a limited space.

Four different styles supported by default are: contactadd, detaildisclose, rowinsert, and rowdelete:

```
<div data-role="view">
  <ul data-role="listview" data-style="inset">
    <li><a>Olympus Has Fallen </a></li>
    <li><a>Jurassic Park 3D</a></li>
    <li><a>G.I. Joe: Retaliation</a></li>
  </ul>

  <ul data-role="listview" data-style="inset">
    <li>Add Contact<a data-role="detailbutton"
      data-style="contactadd"></a></li>
    <li>More Details<a data-role="detailbutton"
      data-style="detaildisclose"></a></li>
    <li>Insert Movie<a data-role="detailbutton"
      data-style="rowinsert"></a></li>
    <li>Delete Movie<a data-role="detailbutton"
      data-style="rowdelete"></a></li>
  </ul>
</div>
```

Try it in jsFiddle:
http://jsfiddle.net/kendomobile/vhXRZ/

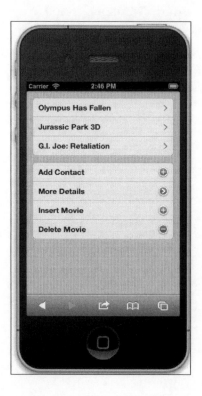

Item icons can also be added to DetailButtons using an `<img>` element or using the `data-icon` attribute for Kendo provided icons. Kendo uses font icons for the icons generated using the `data-icon` attribute. These built-in font icons can be used only inside an anchor tag.

Kendo has the following built-in font icons:

about	action	add	battery	bookmarks
camera	cart	compose	contacts	details
downloads	fastforward	favorites	featured	toprated
globe	history	home	info	more
mostrecent	mostviewed	organize	pause	play
recent	refresh	reply	rewind	search
settings	share	stop	trash	

Custom icons can also be created to be used as button icons. Since the details are outside the scope of this book, we recommend you to go through the Kendo documentation available at the following site: `http://goo.gl/v3yLj`

Grouping and templates

Kendo ListView can be configured to organize items into groups with headers for each group. This is done by setting the type property to `group`:

```
<div data-role="view">
  <ul data-role="listview" data-type="group">
    <li>
      Horror
      <ul>
        <li>Evil Dead</li>
        <li>Scream</li>
        <li>Dark Skies  </li>
      </ul>
    </li>
    <li>
      Sci-Fi
      <ul>
        <li>Prometheus</li>

      </ul>
    </li>
  </ul>
</div>
```

The headers can be made fixed by setting the `fixedHeaders` property to `true`. While scrolling, fixed headers hold their position until all the items under them are scrolled up.

Kendo templates can be used to customize the list items. While implementing templates with ListView, keep in mind that the ListView automatically wraps the template content in a `<li>` tag. Adding a `<li>` tag in the template definition will mess up your ListView, and so only the items that need to be inside `<li>` `</li>` should be in the template. Let's see how easy it is to create a templated ListView with fixed headers and data bound from a DataSource:

```html
<body>

  <div data-role="view" id="mainView" data-init="loadListView">
    <ul id="listView"></ul>
  </div>

  <script type="text/x-kendo-template" id="listviewTemplate">
    <a > <strong > #:movieName# </strong>
    <i>  #:dateTime#</i></a>
  </script>

  <script>

    var app = new kendo.mobile.Application(document.body);

    //create datasource
    var movieDataSource = new kendo.data.DataSource({
      data:
      [
      {
        movieName: "Evil Dead",
        dateTime: "10/7/2013 7:30PM", genre: "Horror"
      },
      {
        movieName: "Scream",
        dateTime: "10/7/2013 8:30PM", genre: "Horror"
      },
      {
        movieName: "Hangover III",
        dateTime: "10/7/2013 9:00PM", genre: "Comedy"
      },
      {
        movieName: "Identity Thief ",
        dateTime: "10/7/2013 1:15PM", genre: "Comedy"
      },
      {
        movieName: "Seven Psychopaths",
```

```
          dateTime: "10/7/2013 4:00PM", genre: "Comedy"
        },
        {
          movieName: "Elysium",
          dateTime: "10/7/2013 7:00PM", genre: "Sci-Fi"
        },
        {
          movieName: "Prometheus",
          dateTime: "10/7/2013 12:45PM", genre: "Sci-Fi"
        }],
        group: "genre"
      });

      //instantiate the list view
      function loadListView() {
        $("#listView").kendoMobileListView({
          dataSource: movieDataSource,
          template: $("#listviewTemplate").html(),
          headerTemplate: "#:value#",
          fixedHeaders: true,
          style: 'inset'
        });
      }
    </script>
  </body>
```

Try it with jsFiddle:
http://jsfiddle.net/kendomobile/n96s2/

To see the scrolling in action in jsFiddle, you may have to reduce your browser's window size so that the list elements in the Result window can scroll.

In this code snippet, we are creating a DataSource object `movieDataSource` using local data and then assigning it to the `dataSource` property of the ListView. We then assign the defined template with the ID `listviewTemplate` to the list for rendering items. `headerTemplate` is set as `#:value#`, which means the value of the property defined in DataSource's `group` property will be displayed as a header. We can add HTML elements also in the header template and treat it just like any other template.

The headers are set to `fixed` and the style is set to `inset`. Here is how the list will look while scrolling:

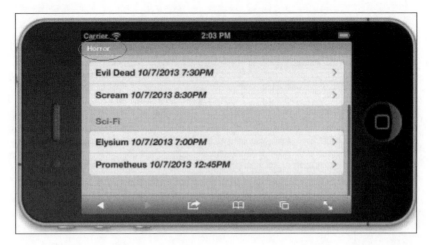

As you can see, the static header will take up the name of the header of the current section as it passes by during scrolling.

The Button widget

We got introduced to Kendo Mobile Button widget in *Chapter 2, Building Your First Mobile Application*. In this chapter we will learn more about this widget and how to customize it. Button is one of the simplest widgets in the Kendo UI Mobile widget stack with a couple of methods and only the click event associated to it. It is used to navigate to a view (local or remote) or to call a JavaScript function when the click event is fired.

Button can be initialized either declaratively using an anchor tag or an HTML5 `<button>` tag by setting the role data attribute:

```
<div data-role="view">
  <br/>
  <button data-role="button" data-click="buttonClick" >
    My Kendo Button
  </button>
  <a data-role="button"  data-click="buttonClick" >
    My Kendo Anchor Button
  </a>
</div>
```

Button is initialized using the jQuery plugin syntax as shown:

```
<a id="kendoButton" >
  Another Button
</a>
var button = $("#kendoButton").kendoMobileButton({
  click: buttonClick
});
```

Try it with jsFiddle:
http://jsfiddle.net/kendomobile/vzsbF/

Icons

Any icon provided by Kendo or your custom icons can be set as the icon attribute's value:

```
var button = $("#kendoButton").kendoMobileButton({
  icon:"globe"
});
```

By default, the icon is displayed first and then the text on the button. If you need the button to be displayed after the text, you can add the following CSS:

```
#kendoButton .km-icon{
  float: right;
  padding-left: 10px;
}
```

The ButtonGroup widget

Sometimes for navigation between sections inside a view, we may need buttons grouped together. The ButtonGroup widget is helpful in this scenario by transforming an HTML list into a set of buttons. Icons can also be set for each individual buttons just like the Button widget.

Initialization

ButtonGroup can be initialized by setting `data-role="buttongroup"` to `<ul> </ul>` as shown in the following code snippet:

```
<ul data-role="buttongroup" >
  <li> Button 1 </li>
  <li> Button 2 </li>
  <li> Button 3 </li>
</ul>
```

ButtonGroup can be initialized using the jQuery plugin syntax too as shown as follows:

```
<div data-role="view" data-init="initialize">
  <ul id="listButtons" >
    <li> button 1 </li>
    <li> button 2 </li>
    <li> button 3 </li>
  </ul>
</div>

<script>
  var app = new kendo.mobile.Application(document.body);
  function initialize(){
    var buttongroup = $("#listButtons").kendoMobileButtonGroup();
  }
</script>
```

Styling

ButtonGroup can be styled in the following two ways:

- Adding your style definitions in the `<li>` element for each button:

```
<ul id="listButtons" data-role="buttongroup" >
  <li style="background-color:green;
    color:white;
    font-style:italic">
    button 1
  </li>
  <li> button 2 </li>
  <li style="background-color:orange;
    color:white;">
    button 3
  </li>
</ul>
```

- Overriding Kendo-generated CSS styles for iOS:

```css
.km-root .km-ios .km-buttongroup .km-button
{
    background-color: red;
}

.km-root .km-ios .km-buttongroup .km-button .km-text
{
    color: white;
}
```

Try it in jsFiddle:
http://jsfiddle.net/kendomobile/XUke5/

Styling individual <li> elements is suited to style buttons individually, and overriding Kendo styles works best when all the buttons are to be styled differently from the default Kendo style.

ButtonGroup in action

Now let's write some code and see the ButtonGroup widget in action by exploring its properties, methods, and events. Our code is going to create a ButtonGroup with four buttons and once a button is selected, we will write to the console the text and index of the button and change the text of the button to `I am clicked`. The buttons will be configured so that a button will be selected only when we release a press on it, which will make sure that, while scrolling, touching the button group will not select a button accidentally. We will also configure the widget so that the buttons are `green` in color by default and once a button is selected, it will change its color to `maroon`:

```html
<body>
  <div data-role="view" data-init="initialize">
    <div>
      <ul id="btnGroup">

        <li>button 1 </li>

        <li>button 2 </li>

        <li>button 3 </li>
      </ul>
```

```
    </div>
  </div>

  <script>

    var app = new kendo.mobile.Application(document.body);
    function initialize() {

      $("#btnGroup").kendoMobileButtonGroup({
        index: 1,
        selectOn: "up",
        select: onButtonSelect
      });
    }

    function onButtonSelect(e) {

      console.log('selected button text was : '
        + this.current().text());
      console.log(" index:" + this.current().index());

      //Change the text on the selected button
      this.current().text('I am clicked');

    }
  </script>
</body>

<style>
  #btnGroup .km-button
  {
    background-color: green;
    color: white;
  }

  #btnGroup .km-state-active
  {
    background-color: maroon;

  }

</style>
```

Try it in jsFiddle:
http://jsfiddle.net/kendomobile/xJ8JB/

During the initialization we are using a couple of properties of the ButtonGroup widget:

- index: This property selects a button with the specified index from the group.

- selectOn: Using this property, we can specify whether the button will be selected as soon as the button is pressed or when the user releases the pressed button. Allowed values are up and down (default). Setting the value of this property to up selects the button selection on the touchend, mouseup, and MSPointerUp platform-specific events, while down does the selection on the touchstart, mousedown, or MSPointerDown events.

Then we hooked up the select event to the onButtonSelect function. Inside this function we read the text on the button using this.current().text(). The current() method will return the currently selected button's jQuery object. Similarly we found the index of the currently selected button using this.current().index(). Once the current button's data is read using jQuery's text() method, the text of the button is changed.

To set the initial color of the buttons, we updated the style provided by the .km-button CSS class. The .km-state-active class styles the currently selected button. By setting the background color to maroon in this class, we changed the selected button's background color.

We can also use ButtonGroup's select(index) method to select a button with the index provided as input.

The Switch widget

Switch is a common UI element on mobile devices which is used for binary on/off or true/false data input. The Switch widget can either be tapped or dragged to toggle its value.

The Kendo Mobile Switch widget is created by transforming an HTML checkbox. The checked property will get or set the checked/unchecked state of the widget. The label for a checked state is set using the onLabel property and the offLabel property sets the unchecked state's label.

The `check()` method gets and sets the checked state of the widget and the `toggle()` method toggles the checked state. When the checked state of the widget is changed, the change event is fired.

Initialization

Now let's see different ways of initializing the Switch widget:

Data attribute initialization by setting `data-role="switch"`:

```
<input type="checkbox" id="chkSwitch1"
  data-role="switch" checked="checked"
    data-on-label="Pass"
      data-off-label="Fail" />
```

jQuery plugin syntax:

```
<div data-role="view" data-init="init">
  <input type="checkbox" id="chkSwitch2"  />
</div>

<script>
  var app = new kendo.mobile.Application(document.body);
  function init(){
    $('#chkSwitch2').kendoMobileSwitch({
      checked:false,
      onLabel:'Yes',
      offLabel:'No'
    });
  }

</script>
```

Try it in jsFiddle:
http://jsfiddle.net/kendomobile/vk5XW/

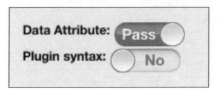

The Pane widget

The Pane widget is used to group multiple views within the main view of the Kendo Mobile application. It acts like an app inside an app by allowing navigation to remote/local views, transition effects, layouts, setting default views, specific loading text, and so on. Pane is used by widgets such as PopOver and SplitView to accommodate multiple views inside them.

The Pane widget is initialized by setting the role data attribute to `pane`:

```
<div data-role="pane">
  <div data-role="view" id="view1">
    I am the 1st view
  </div>
  <div data-role="view" id="bar">
    I am the 2nd view
  </div>
</div>
```

Methods

The `hideLoading` and `showLoading` methods hide and show the loading animation set by the loading configuration property of the Pane widget. The `view()` method gives the reference to the current view loaded on the pane.

Just like the Kendo application object, the Pane widget also has a `navigate(url, transition)` method which navigates to views both inside and outside of the pane. Different transition effects can be provided using the transition input configuration.

By default, the pane navigates to views inside the current pane. To navigate to views inside other panes, the target data attribute is set to the external pane's ID in the navigational element:

```
<a data-role="button" href="#outsideView"
  data-target="external-pane">External Pane</a>
```

To navigate to other views inside the application (which are not inside panes), the value of the target attribute is set to _top:

```
<a data-role="button" href="#mobileView"
  data-target="_top">Mobile View</a>
```

Events

The Pane widget has two events:

- `navigate(e)`: This event is fired when navigation to a view occurs. The event data contains a `url` property (`e.url`) which has the URL of the navigated view.

- `viewShow(e)`: This event is fired when a view is shown inside the Pane widget. The event data contains a `view` property which has the reference to the loaded view.

The PopOver widget

The PopOver widget is used on tablet devices to display content on a visual layer that floats above the app's window. This widget is typically used in the following scenarios:

- To display some information about an element

- To display a menu for navigating to other views

- To display a context menu with actions to be performed

- To display a filter list

The PopOver widget can contain multiple views inside it and they can be navigated between each other. The views are automatically added inside a Pane widget. The Pane widget's properties can be set using the pane configuration option.

Initialization

The widget can be initialized declaratively by setting `data-role="popover"`. Additional pop-up options can be set through the `data-popup` attribute.

The PopOver widget can be opened by tapping a navigational widget by adding the `data-rel="popover"` attribute and a `href` attribute targeting the PopOver's ID or programmatically by calling its `open()` method:

```
<a data-role="button" href="#popOverWidget"
  data-rel="popover">Filter</a>

<div id="popOverWidget" data-role="popover"
  data-popup="{'height':150}">

  <div data-role="view">
    <ul data-role="listview">
```

```
  <li>
    <a href="#">Comedy (9)</a>

  </li>
  <li>
    <a href="#">Action (10)</a>

  </li>
  <li>
    <a href="#">Romantic (5)</a>

  </li>
  <li>
    <a href="#">War (7)</a>

  </li>
    </ul>
  </div>
</div>
```

The PopOver widget can be initialized using the jQuery plugin syntax as shown in the following code snippet:

```
<div data-role="view" data-init="init">
  <a data-role="button" href="#popOverWidget"
    data-rel="popover">Select Genre</a>
  <div id="popOverWidget" >
    <div data-role="view">
      <ul data-role="listview" >
        <li>
          <a href="#">Comedy (9)</a>
        </li>
        <li>
          <a href="#">Action (10)</a>
        </li>
        <li>
          <a href="#">Romantic (5)</a>
        </li>
      </ul>
    </div>
  </div>
</div>
```

```
<script>
  var app = new kendo.mobile.Application(document.body);

  function init(){
    $('#popOverWidget').kendoMobilePopOver({
      popup: { height: '130px' }
    });


  }
</script>
```

Try it in jsFiddle:
http://jsfiddle.net/kendomobile/cDBur/

PopOver with multiple views

There are many scenarios we encounter where, in a PopOver widget, we need to display multiple views and navigate to each other depending on some condition. A common example is a multiview menu where the entire view is replaced by another level of menu.

Let's see how easily this can be implemented for selecting a movie from a genre list and then from a movie list using the PopOver widget as shown in the following code snippet:

```
<head>
  <style>
    .no-backbutton .km-back {
      visibility: hidden;
    }
  </style>
</head>
<body>
  <div data-role="view" >
    <a data-role="button" href="#popOverWidget"
      data-rel="popover">
      Select Movie
    </a>

    <div id="popOverWidget" data-role="popover"
      data-pane="{'transition':'zoom',
        'layout':'popoverLayout'}"
          data-popup="{'height':170}">

      <!-- Layout -->
      <div data-role="layout" data-id="popoverLayout">
        <div data-role="header">
          <a data-role="backbutton" > Back </a>
        </div>
        <div data-role="footer"></div>
      </div>
      <!-- main menu view-->
      <div data-role="view" id="view-main"
        class="no-backbutton" >
        <ul data-role="listview" >
          <li><a href="#view-comedy">Comedy (3)</a></li>
          <li><a href="#view-action">Action (2)</a></li>
        </ul>
      </div>
      <!-- Comedy Menu View-->
      <div data-role="view" id="view-comedy">
        <ul data-role="listview" >
          <li>
            <a href="#view-final?movie=Hangover III">
              Hangover III
            </a>
          </li>
          <li>
            <a href="#view-final?movie=Scary Movie">
              Scary Movie
            </a>
```

```
              </li>
              <li>
                <a href="#view-final?movie=Ted">Ted </a>
              </li>
            </ul>
          </div>
          <!-- Action Menu View-->
          <div data-role="view" id="view-action">
            <ul data-role="listview" >
              <li>
                <a href="#view-final?movie=Iron Man 3">
                  Iron Man 3
                </a>
              </li>
              <li>
                <a href="#view-final?movie=After Earth">
                  After Earth
                </a>
              </li>
            </ul>
          </div>
          <!-- Final View-->
          <div data-role="view" id="view-final"
            data-show="finalViewShow">
            <div>
              <h3>You selected: </h3>
              <h2>
                <!-- Selected movie name will be
                  displayed in this span -->
                <span id="spanMovieName"> </span>

              </h2>
            </div>
          </div>
        </div>
      </div>
    <script>
    var app = new kendo.mobile.Application(document.body);

    //Function to be called when the view is shown every time
    function finalViewShow(e) {

      //show the movie name in the view
      $('#spanMovieName').text(e.view.params.movie);
    }
    </script>
</body>
```

Try it in jsFiddle:
`http://jsfiddle.net/kendomobile/ffjVh/`

We added three views in the PopOver widget, two menus, and one final view, where the selected movie is displayed. The menus are assigned a common layout (popoverLayout) which contains a header element with a Kendo BackButton widget. The back button is hidden in the first view using the following CSS class as we did in *Chapter 2, Building Your First Mobile Application*:

```
.no-backbutton .km-back { visibility: hidden; }
```

For all other views, the back button is visible and by using it we can navigate to the previous view.

In the view with ID `view-main`, we are showing the genre of the movies, and clicking on the links will take you to the appropriate movie menu views, that is, `view-comedy` or `view-action`. In this menu, we are displaying movies as links with the movie name passed to the view with ID `view-final` as a query string. Once we click a movie name and navigate to the final view, the function `finalViewShow` is invoked. This function reads the movie name from the query string and displays it on the view.

 We are calling the `finalViewShow` function inside the `show` event and not in the `init` event as we need the function to be invoked every time the view is displayed. The `init` function will be invoked only once when the view is initialized.

The second and third view of the PopOver widget we created is shown as follows:

 Kendo provides a drag-and-drop ThemeBuilder using which you can theme widgets to match your app's look and feel. The mobile ThemeBuilder can be accessed using this URL: `http://demos.kendoui.com/mobilethemebuilder/index.html`

Summary

In this chapter, we explored the basics of Kendo UI Mobile widgets and learned about commonly available methods. We then took a deep dive into widgets such as ListView, Button, ButtonGroup, Switch, Pane, and PopOver and saw how to instantiate them and use them in multiple scenarios using examples available on jsFiddle. Some undocumented tips about tweaking the widgets were also discussed. In the next chapter we will explore more Kendo UI Mobile widgets.

6
ActionSheet, ModalView, and More Widgets

In the previous chapter, we learned the basics of Kendo UI Mobile widgets and explored quite a few of them. In this chapter, we will continue the momentum and explore even more widgets hands-on using jsFiddle examples. By the end of this chapter, you will be an expert in using all the Kendo UI Mobile widgets and we will be ready to integrate the widgets in our Movie Tickets application.

In this chapter we will cover:

- ActionSheet
- ModalView
- SplitView
- Scroller
- ScrollView
- Touch
- Drawer

The ActionSheet widget

Action sheets are used on mobile devices (typically on mobile phones) to display multiple options to the user for an action. They contain multiple buttons with a text for each action. A typical action sheet is displayed as shown in the following screenshot:

Kendo UI Mobile's ActionSheet widget provides this functionality by transforming a <ul> to an action sheet and calling a preconfigured function when the items on the sheet are clicked. ActionSheet can be opened with a tap in any other widget if we set the data-rel="actionsheet" and href attributes as the ActionSheet's element ID prefixed with a hash (#).

Initialization

ActionSheet can be initialized declaratively as shown in the following code:

```
<div data-role="view">

<a data-role="button" data-rel="actionsheet"
    id="tnShare " href="#confirmationSheet">
    Share
</a>

  <ul data-role="actionsheet"
      id="confirmationSheet">
```

```
<li>
    <a data-action="shareOnTwitter">
        Twitter
    </a>
</li>
<li>
    <a data-action="shareOnFB">
        Facebook
    </a>
</li>
<li>
    <a data-action="justEmail">
        Email
    </a>
</li>

    </ul>
</div>
```

Initialization, using the jQuery plugin syntax can be done as shown in the following code snippet:

```
<div data-role="view">

<a data-role="button" id="btnShare"
        data-rel="actionsheet"
        href="#confirmationSheet">Share</a>

<ul id="confirmationSheet">
        <li>
            <a data-action="shareOnTwitter">Twitter
            </a>
        </li>
        <li>
            <a data-action="shareOnFB">Facebook
            </a>
        </li>
        <li>
            <a data-action="justEmail">Email
            </a>
        </li>
    </ul>
</div>
```

```
<script>
    var app = new kendo.mobile.Application(document.body);
    function initialize() {
        $("#confirmationSheet").kendoMobileActionSheet();

    }

function shareOnTwitter(e){
    console.log('twitter...');
    console.log(e.target);
}

function shareOnFB(e){
    console.log('FB...');
    console.log(e.target);

}

function justEmail(e){
    console.log('Email...');
    console.log(e.target);

}
</script>
```

Try it in jsFiddle:

`http://jsfiddle.net/kendomobile/Zn4eW/`

`http://jsfiddle.net/kendomobile/5HQkr/`

The widget can also be opened programmatically by calling its open method. The click event of the buttons in the ActionSheet widget can be attached to a function using the data-action attribute. A **Cancel** action button is automatically added to the bottom of the sheet.

The previous code is rendered differently in different platforms. In iPhone, the widget slides up from the bottom as a modal dialog box, whereas in iPad it is rendered in a **PopOver** widget. The following screenshots are from iPhone and iPad respectively:

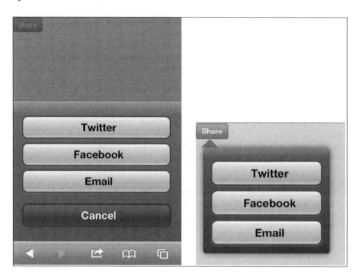

 The autogenerated **Cancel** button's text can be changed by setting the cancel option of the widget as in the following script:

```
<ul data-role="actionsheet" data-cancel="Custom Text"
    id="confirmationSheet">

        <li>.... </li>
</ul>
```

Actions

The functions wired to the click of the `action` buttons receive an object as an input.

This object has two parameters:

- `target`: This is a jQuery object of the HTML element, which opened the ActionSheet widget. In our example, it's the Button widget `$('btnShare')`.

- `context`: This is the value that is set using the `data-actionsheet-context` attribute of the widget. This parameter is optional and can be used to identify which widget has been opened when there are multiple action sheets defined in a view.

Open and close

The ActionSheet widget can be programmatically opened by invoking the open method.

The open() method takes two input parameters:

- target: This is a jQuery object of the HTML element which is available in the action functions. This object is optional for mobile phones but is required for tablets as the positioning of the widget depend on the target element.
- context: This is an optional value which is available as the context property in the action function's input parameter.

The widget can be closed using the close() method. The close() method has no input parameters:

```
$("#confirmationSheet").data("kendoMobileActionSheet").close();
```

On tablets, the ActionSheet widget opens as a popped-up widget. The direction of opening, height, and weight properties of the widget can be configured using the pop-up properties of the ActionSheet widget.

The ModalView widget

The Kendo Mobile **ModalView** widget opens up a view as a child window, which requires the user to interact with it before returning to the main application view. It is typically used to grab the user's full attention by asking the user to enter some detail or to display very important information. Typical scenarios are customized error/confirmation messages, password entry box, and so on.

The ModalView widget can be defined inside or outside of a view and it can have its own layout. It is recommended to reduce the use of ModalView to the minimum in mobile apps as users will be interrupted from their workflow and creates exasperating experience closing trivial modal windows.

The widget's height and width can be defined using the data-height and data-width attributes. To open the widget programmatically, we can use the open() method after getting the reference of the widget using the jQuery data method. An event handler function can be attached to the open event of ModalView by wiring it using the data-open attribute.

Initializaton

A ModalView widget can be initialized declaratively using data attributes as shown in the following code:

```
<div data-role="view">
    <a href="#myModalView" data-rel="modalview"
        data-role="button">
            Open Modal View
    </a>
</div>

<div data-role="modalview" data-height="300px"
      data-width="300px"
      id="myModalView">
    <h2> I am a modal view... </h2>
</div>
```

It can also be initialized using the jQuery plugin syntax:

```
<div data-role="view" data-init="init">
    <a href="#myModalView" data-rel="modalview"
        data-role="button">
            Open Modal View
    </a>
</div>

<div id="myModalView">
    <h2> Modal View... </h2>
</div>

<script>
var app = new kendo.mobile.Application(document.body);
function init(){
    $('#myModalView').kendoMobileModalView({
                    height:100,width:100
            }).data("kendoMobileModalView");

}
</script>
```

Try it in jsFiddle:

http://jsfiddle.net/kendomobile/29cdw/

http://jsfiddle.net/kendomobile/SZysp/

Opening the widget

The ModalView widget can be opened using the open() method. An event can be fired at the time of opening the widget, which can be attached using the data-open attribute demonstrated in the sample code of the next section.

The following code snippet opens a ModalView widget:

```
<div data-role="view">
    <a data-click="openModalView"
        data-role="button">
            Open Modal View
    </a>
</div>

<div data-role="modalview"
    data-height="300px"
    data-width="300px"
    id="myModalView">
    <h2> I am a modal view... </h2>

</div>
<script>
function openModalView(e) {
            $("#myModalView").data("kendoMobileModalView").open();
        }
</script>
```

 Try it in jsFiddle:
http://jsfiddle.net/kendomobile/Y5WcN/

Closing the widget

The widget can be closed using the close method. An event can be fired at the time of closing the widget which can be attached using the data-close attribute.

The following code snippet opens a ModalView widget programmatically and fires the events during opening and closing of the widget. Inside the widget, there is a **Close Me !** button which, when clicked, closes the widget using the `data("kendoMobileModalView").close()` method:

```
<div data-role="view">
    <a data-rel="modalview"
        href="#myModalView"
        data-role="button">
        Open Modal View
    </a>
</div>

  <div data-role="modalview" data-open="modalViewOpen"
        data-close="modalViewClose" data-height="200px"
        data-width="300px"id="myModalView">

    <a style="float:right" data-click="closeModalView"
        data-role="button">
            Close Me !
    </a>
    <h2> I am a modal view... </h2>
</div>

<script>
    var app = new kendo.mobile.Application(document.body);

  function modalViewOpen(e){

      console.log('widget opened');
  }

  function modalViewClose(e){
      console.log('widget closed');
  }

  function closeModalView(e){
  $("#myModalView").data("kendoMobileModalView").close();
  }

</script>
```

Try it in jsFiddle:
http://jsfiddle.net/kendomobile/6wPXA/

 By setting `data-modal='false'`, the ModalView widget can also be closed by tapping outside of the window:

```
$('#myModalView').kendoMobileModalView({
        modal:false,
        }).data("kendoMobileModalView");
```

The SplitView widget

On tablet devices, we have a lot of space compared to mobile phones and rarely do we take the entire space for a UI element as with mobile phones. The SplitView widget allows us to divide a tablet's screen up into multiple sections using the pane widgets, and display different views in each P ane. This widget is typically used to display navigation on the left-hand side, and a detail view on the right-hand side. See the following classic example of a split view – iPad **Settings** screen:

A SplitView widget is not added inside a view unlike other Kendo Mobile widgets, and should be added independently just like a view in your local- or remote-view file. A SplitView widget should contain only panes as child elements with views defined in panes.

Initialization

The SplitView widget is initialized by setting the attribute `data-role="splitview"` as shown in the following code snippet:

```
<div data-role="splitview" >
  <div data-role="pane" >
    <div data-role="view" >
        <h1>Left Pane </h1>
    </div>
  </div>

  <div data-role="pane" >
    <div data-role="view" >
        <h1>Right Pane </h1>
    </div>
  </div>
</div>
```

The jQuery plugin syntax for this example is:

```
<div id="kendoSplitView" >
  <div data-role="pane" >
    <div data-role="view" >
        <h1>Left Pane </h1>
    </div>
  </div>

  <div data-role="pane" >
    <div data-role="view" >
        <h1>Right Pane </h1>
    </div>
  </div>
</div>
<script>
var app = new kendo.mobile.Application(document.body);
$('#kendoSplitView').kendoMobileSplitView().
data("kendoMobileSplitView");
</script>
```

Try it in jsFiddle:

http://jsfiddle.net/kendomobile/TFcZ7/

http://jsfiddle.net/kendomobile/p3Hgp/

Setting the `style` property to vertical (`data-style="vertical"`) will make the SplitView stacked up vertically. The default value for the `style` configuration is `horizontal`.

SplitView in action

SplitView can be used to create very complex UI structures, with multiple panes and multiple views inside each pane. Let's create a simple SplitView that will work as a starting point for building complex UI structures. In this example, we are creating a split view with two panes and one view in each pane. The first pane on the left side will act as a master pane, which displays a list of genres. When we click/tap on one of the list items, the selected genre is sent to the detail/right-side pane as a query string within the view's URL and displayed on the detail view:

```
<div data-role="splitview" >

    <div data-role="pane" >
        <!-- Master view -->
        <div data-role="view" data-title="Genre" >
            <ul data-role="listview" data-style=="inset">
                <li>
                    <a href="#view-detail?genre=Drama"
                        data-target="pane-detail"> Drama </a>
                </li>
                <li>
                    <a href="#view-detail?genre=Horror"
                        data-target="pane-detail">Horror </a>
                </li>
                <li>
                    <a href="#view-detail?genre=Family"
                        data-target="pane-detail">Family </a>
                </li>
                <li>
                    <a href="#view-detail?genre=History"
                        data-target="pane-detail">History </a>
                </li>
            </ul>

        </div>
    </div>

    <div data-role="pane" id="pane-detail" >
        <!-- Detail view -->
        <div data-role="view" id="view-detail"
            style="font-size:16px"
            data-show="detailViewShown" >
```

```
<div style="padding:10px;">
<strong >Selected Genre:   </strong>
<strong>
    <!--Selected genre will be written here -->
    <span id="selected-genre"
            style="color:green"> </span>
</strong>
</div>

    </div>
  </div>
</div>
<script>
var app = new kendo.mobile.Application(document.body);

function detailViewShown(e){
    //Read the selected genre from the query string
    $('#view-detail #selected-genre').text(e.view.params.genre);
}
</script>
```

Try it in jsFiddle:
http://jsfiddle.net/kendomobile/G3Edm/

We created a SplitView and defined two panes inside it. The pane with the ID pane-detail acts as the detail pane and inside this pane we have defined a view with the ID view-detail. Every list item in the master view pane has a link to the detail view with the genre added in the query string, and by setting the attribute as data-target="pane-detail", we are telling the pane to search for matching views inside the pane with the ID pane-detail.

In the show event of the view, we are calling the function detailViewShown(). This function reads the genre from the selected query string available in the parameters collection e.view.params, and updates the text inside the span with the ID selected-genre.

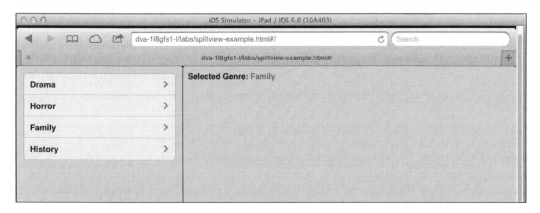

When there are two panes in the SplitView widget, it automatically renders with left pane - right pane ratio as 1:2. There is a bug in Kendo UI Mobile 2013.1.319 Version, which reverses the ratio to 2:1; so you may have to use a later version of the framework to see the correct behavior of the SplitView widget.

The Scroller widget

The **Scroller** widget helps in creating a touch-sensitive and scrollable section in the DOM with fixed width and/or height. It can be initialized by setting the `data-role="scroller"` attribute in the wrapper element or programmatically using the jQuery plugin syntax in the containing view's `init` event as shown in the following code snippet:

```
<div id="scrollableContents"> </div>
  $("# scrollableContents ").kendoMobileScroller();
```

A Kendo view widget, by default, wraps its contents inside in a Scroller widget, and so, we should use this widget only for specific scrollable sections inside the view. The widget can be accessed inside the view events using the `e.view.scroller` property where `e` is the input object of the event.

Configurations

Here are some of the commonly used Scroller configurations:

- `useNative`: Native scrolling on the platform is enabled when this property is set to `true`. The default value is `false`.
- `elastic`: This property has an enable or disable elastic behavior while crossing Scroller bounds. By default the property is set to `true`.
- `zoom`: Using the pinch zoom gesture, the contents inside the Scroller widget can be zoomed in or out. The default value is `false`.

 If the native scroller supports elastic scrolling by default, the Scrolling will be elastic even if elastic is set to `false` when `useNative` is set to `true`.

Pull to refresh

The **Pull-to-refresh** feature is built into the Scroller widget, which is useful to update the contents for an entire view or section by section basis. It can be enabled in a Scroller widget by setting the `pullToRefresh` property to `true`. Along with `pullToRefresh`, we can set the following properties too for customizing the pull-to-refresh experience:

- `pullOffset`: The `pull` event is fired (in this event's handler function we write the code to update the Scroller contents) when the user pulls beyond the `pullOffset` value. The default value is `140`.
- `pullTemplate`: The HTML template is displayed when the user pulls the Scroller inside the boundary set by `pullOffset`.
- `releaseTemplate`: An HTML template is displayed when the user pulls the Scroller beyond the boundary set by `pullOffset`.
- `refreshTemplate`: The HTML template displayed while the data is updated in the Scroller. This template is removed only when the `pullHandled()` method is called.

 The Scroller options can be set only using JavaScript code in the view's `init` event and not declaratively using data attributes, as the Scroller widget is not exposed by itself. The mobile view instantiates the Scroller around its contents.

The `pullHandled()` method removes the contents in the refresh template and positions the updated contents into the initial view.

Now let's write some code to create a Scroller widget with the pull-to-refresh feature. The scrollable content contains a number and when the user pulls and releases the Scroller, a random number between 1 and 1000 replaces the previous number:

```
<body>
    <div data-role="view" data-init="viewInit">

        <div id="scrollSection" data-zoom="true"
            data-role="scroller"
            style="height: 200px;text-align: center;">
            <span id="scrollContent"
                    style="font-size: 150px;">100
            </span>
        </div>
    </div>
    <script>
        var app = new kendo.mobile.Application(document.body);

        function viewInit(e) {
            //get reference of the scroller
            var scroller = $("#scrollSection")
                            .data("kendoMobileScroller");

            //set scroller options
            scroller.setOptions({
                pullToRefresh: true,
                //pull event is fired when user pulls beyond
                //value set using pullOffset
                pull: refresh,
                //set the boundary after which the pull will
                //fire the pull event default value is 140
                pullOffset: 100,
                pullTemplate: "<i>Pull to update the number</i>",
                releaseTemplate: "Release to update the number",
                refreshTemplate: "Updating..."
            });
        }

        function refresh() {

            //create a random number between 1 and 1000
            var newNumber = Math.floor(
                            , (Math.random() * 1000) + 1);
            var scroller =
```

```
                    $("#scrollSection").data("kendoMobileScroller");
        //update the contents inside the scroller
        scroller.scrollElement.find('#scrollContent')
                          .text(newNumber);

        //pullHandled method removes the contents
        //in the refresh template and positions the u
        //updated contents to the initial view
        scroller.pullHandled();
    }

  </script>
</body>
```

 Try it in jsFiddle:
http://jsfiddle.net/kendomobile/2WJhE/

The ScrollView widget

The **ScrollView** widget is useful to display a wide image, contents with multiple horizontal pages as in a picture gallery, or a series of instructions which can be accessed page-by-page and so on, using the swipe gesture. The ScrollView widget can be initialized by setting the role data attribute to scrollview (data-role= "scrollview") or programmatically using the jQuery plugin syntax that invokes $("#scrollViewMain").kendoMobileScrollView() in the HTML, where scrollViewMain is the ID of the HTML element on which the ScrollView widget is initialized.

Pages can be defined inside the ScrollView with the role data attribute set as "page" (data-role= "page"). Contents in a page are displayed one by one in a sequential manner when the user swipes through the ScrollView. Extra white spaces between the page HTML elements will appear as pages in the ScrollView, and this is why we need to make sure that the HTML elements defining the pages are continuous without any white spaces in between, as shown in the following code:

```
<div data-role="view">
    <div id="myScrollView" data-role="scrollview">
        <div data-role="page">Page 1 </div><div
    data-role="page">Page 2</div><div
    data-role="page">Page 3</div><div
    data-role="page">Page 4</div>
    </div>
</div>
```

Kendo automatically adds the following CSS class to the element on which ScrollView is initialized:

```
.km-scrollview {
white-space: nowrap;
overflow: hidden;
width: 100%;
}
```

Because of the CSS property white-space: nowrap, long texts inside pages will spill to other pages. To keep the text inside each page wrapped inside the page itself, we need to use the following style:

```
.km-scrollview > div > [data-role=page] {
        white-space: pre-wrap;        /*or normal*/
        }
```

Now let's create a ScrollView with three pages of tips about the ScrollView widget itself:

```html
<head>
<style>
        .km-scrollview > div > [data-role=page] {
            /*This is to preserve whitespace.
             Text will wrap when necessary, and on line breaks*/
            white-space: pre-wrap;
            /*normal can also be used instead of pre-wrap*/
        }
    </style>
</head>
<body>
    <div data-role="view">

        <div data-role="scrollview" data-duration="3000"
            data-change="pageChange"
            style="padding-top: 15px;">
            <div data-role="page">
                <h1>Tip1</h1>

            In ScrollView, remove all white spaces
        between page HTML elements. Otherwise,
        white spaces will appear as pages in
        the rendered ScrollView.

            </div><div data-role="page">
                <h1>Tip2 </h1>

            You can set the time taken in milliseconds
        by the ScrollView to settle down the current
        page after the using the duration property.

            </div><div data-role="page">
                <h1>Tip3 </h1>

            scrollTo() method can be used to navigate
        to a specific page in the ScrollView.
            </div></div>
    </div>
    <script>
        var app = new kendo.mobile.Application(document.body);
        function pageChange(e) {
            //logs the current page number.
            console.log(e.page);
        }
    </script>
</body>
```

Try it in jsFiddle:
http://jsfiddle.net/kendomobile/6JxRU/

In the previous code, we created three pages in the ScrollView with tips and set the
`data-duration` attribute to `3000` milliseconds, which is the animation time for the
current page to settle down. We also hooked the `pageChange()` function as the event
handler for the `change` event, which is fired when the user is navigated to a page.

If you would like to remove the page indicators at the bottom of the
ScrollView, the following CSS will do the trick:

```
.km-pages > li {
        display:none;
}
```

The Touch widget

Kendo UI Mobile's **Touch** widget helps us make selected elements of the DOM sensitive to a user's touch. It's a very powerful component as we don't need to use Mobile widgets wherever actions need to be implemented for touch events. Just add data-role = "touch" on the HTML element and we are ready to trap events such as swipe, tap, double tap, hold, and more:

```
<div id="touchableDiv" data-role="touch"> </div>
```

Or

```
$("#touchableDiv").kendoTouch();
```

Now let's see how the touch events can be trapped and what kind of data we can extract on a touch-enabled div element with an inner div element. Every touch event handler receives an event object, and in this example, we are going to explore some important properties that can be retrieved from the event object.

Let's create the following HTML with a couple of div elements:

```
<div data-role="view" data-init="viewInit">
    <div id="touchableDiv"
        style="height: 200px; width: 200px;
            background-color: darkgreen;">

        <div style="height: 100px; width: 100px;
            background-color: white;"
            id="innerDiv">
        </div>
    </div>
</div>
```

Next, in JavaScript code, let's initialize the div with the ID touchableDiv as a Touch widget in the init event of the view. A single event handler is defined for all the touch events and the properties are written to the console of your browser. The description of each of the used properties is added as comments in the following code:

```
<script>
    var app = new kendo.mobile.Application(document.body);
    function viewInit(e) {

        $('#touchableDiv').kendoTouch({

            tap: handleTouchEvent,
```

```
            doubletap: handleTouchEvent,
            hold: handleTouchEvent,
            touchstart: handleTouchEvent,
            touchend: handleTouchEvent,
            dragstart: handleTouchEvent,
            dragend: handleTouchEvent
        });
    }

    function handleTouchEvent(e) {
        console.log(e);

        //Touch properties

        //id of the actual HTML element
        //which was touched. if we touch the div
        //with id innerDiv, output will be 'innerDiv'
        console.log("actual touch on: " +
            e.touch.initialTouch.id);

        //parent touch widget which was touched.
        console.log("current target id: " +
            e.touch.currentTarget.id);
        //Touch offset relative to the entire document
        console.log("x.location: " + e.touch.x.location +
            " y.location: " + e.touch.y.location);
        //Touch offset relative to the viewport
        console.log("x.client: " + e.touch.x.client +
            " y.client: " + e.touch.y.client);
        //Velocity of the touch event in pixels
        // per millisecond.
        console.log("x.velocity: " + e.touch.x.velocity +
            " y.velocity: " + e.touch.y.velocity);

        //Epoch timestamp
        console.log("x.timeStamp: " + e.touch.x.timeStamp +
            " y.timeStamp: " + e.touch.y.timeStamp);

        //Event Properties
        console.log("Event Type: " + e.event.type);
    }

    </script>
</body>
```

Try it in jsFiddle:
http://jsfiddle.net/kendomobile/J6xmr/

In the fiddle, we are writing the output to the div element in the UI, but if you write the output to your Chrome browser console, you can see the output as shown in the following screenshot:

```
▼ Object {touch: d.extend.init, event: b.Event, sender: n.extend.init, _de]
    _defaultPrevented: false
  ▶ event: b.Event
  ▶ isDefaultPrevented: function (){return this._defaultPrevented===!0}
  ▶ preventDefault: function (){this._defaultPrevented=!0}
  ▶ sender: n.extend.init
  ▶ touch: d.extend.init
  ▶ __proto__: Object
actual touch on: innerDiv
current target id: touchableDiv
x.location: 51 y.location: 68
x.client: 51 y.client: 68
x.velocity: 0 y.velocity: 0
x.timeStamp: 1367530287218 y.timeStamp: 1367530287218
Event Type: mousedown
```

The Swipe event

Horizontal swipe can be enabled in a Touch widget by setting the attribute as enableSwipe="true", which will trigger the swipe event. For this event, the following properties can be configured:

- maxDuration: This property defines the lifetime of a swipe event in milliseconds. The default value is set to 1 second. Swipe is discarded if the event is not completed within this time frame.

- minXDelta: This property is the minimum horizontal pixels that need to be traversed to fore the swipe event. The default value is set to 30.

- minYDelta: This is the maximum deviation allowed vertically. The default value is set to 20. This means if the swipe goes down or up more than 20 pixels, it will be discarded.

- surface: This is the element's jQuery object on which the swipe/drag can be extended. This property can be used to extend the swipe surface area to bigger parent elements so as to provide a better user experience.

When the enableSwipe option is set to true, all the drag events dragstart, drag, and dragend events will be disabled as they are mutually exclusive events.

```
<div data-role="view" data-init="viewInit">
        <div id="parentDiv"
            style="height: 300px; width: 300px;
                background-color: darkgreen;">

            <div style="height: 200px; width: 200px;
                background-color: white;"
                id="touchableDiv">
            </div>
        </div>
    <div id="eventLog">
    </div>
</div>
<script>
var app = new kendo.mobile.Application(document.body);

function viewInit(e){

    $('#touchableDiv').kendoTouch({
        enableSwipe:true,
        swipe:swipeEvent,
        minXDelta: 50,
        maxYDelta:40,
        maxDuration:2000
    });
}

function swipeEvent(e){
    $('#eventLog').append('Swipe registered....' +
                        'Direction: ' + e.direction
                        + '<br/>');

}
</script>
```

> Try it in jsFiddle:
> http://jsfiddle.net/kendomobile/r2fYv/

The previous code will capture swipes in the inner div and logs the swipe direction on the screen.

Multi-touch gestures

By setting the Touch widget's `multi-touch` property to `true`, Multi-touch (currently only two-finger gestures are supported) gestures can be enabled. The events fired while performing Multi-touch are `gesturestart`, `gesturechange`, and `gestureend` in the same order. These events' event object input parameter has additional properties compared to other touch events:

- `touches`: An array containing two active touch objects; one for each touch
- `distance`: The distance between the two touches in pixels
- `Center`: The center point between the two touches, `center.x` and `center.y` provides the co-ordinates.

The Drawer widget

The Drawer widget, commonly known as the Facebook-style side menu, was introduced in the 2013 Q2 release of Kendo UI. This menu style has nowadays turned into a standard for any mobile application that has a lot of content and a complex navigation stack.

The Drawer widget can be initialized by setting the `data-role="drawer"` attribute to a `div` element. By default, the widget appears from the left side on a left-to-right swipe. The drawer can be made to slide in from right to left, by setting the `position` data attribute to `right`:

```
data-position="right";
```

The drawer slides back in when we navigate to another view or an opposite swipe gesture is done by the user. The widget also supports adding a custom header and footer; this feature is optional.

Let's now implement a drawer containing a `ListView`, which slides in from right to left:

```
<div data-role="drawer" id="right-drawer"
    data-position="right" >
  <ul data-role="listview" data-type="group">
      <li>Menu
          <ul>
```

```
        <li data-icon="camera">
            Take Photo
        </li>
        <li data-icon="globe">
            Browse
        </li>

    </ul>
</li>
<li>Account
    <ul>
        <li data-icon="delete">
            Delete
        </li>
        <li data-icon="about">
            About
        </li>
    </ul>
</li>
    </ul>
</div>

 <div data-role="view" id="view1"
     data-title="View 1">
        <div>
            Swipe from right to left to
            view the Drawer widget
        </div>
</div>
</div>
```

Try it in jsFiddle:
http://jsfiddle.net/kendomobile/sCb56/

When swiped from right to left, the drawer is displayed on the view with the items in the ListView as shown in the following set of screenshots:

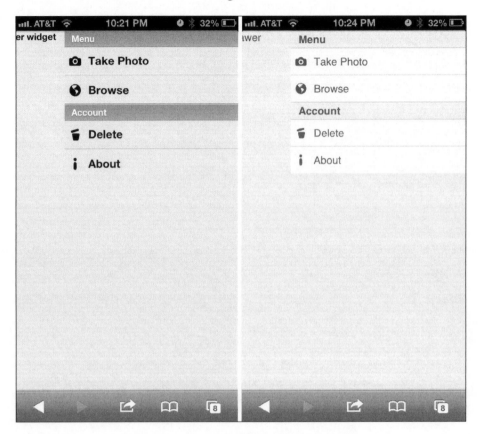

Enabling and disabling Drawer on specific views

The Drawer widget can be configured so that it is enabled for certain views only. This is achieved by providing the view IDs as an array to the `views` data attribute:

```
<div data-role="drawer" data-views="[view1', 'view2']">
</div>
```

If the `views` data attribute is not configured, the widget will be displayed for all the views in the mobile app.

If you have a lot of views and you just want to hide the Drawer, only for a few views, then go to the beforeShow event of the widget, and check for the currently loaded view ID and call the preventDefault() method so that the Drawer is not shown.

Let's modify the previous example to see it in action:

```
<div data-role="drawer" id="right-drawer"
        data-position="right"
        data-before-show="onBeforeShow">
    <ul data-role="listview" data-type="group">
        <li>Menu
        <ul>
            <li data-icon="camera">
                <a href="#view1">Take Photo </a>
            </li>
            <li data-icon="globe">
                <a href="#view2">Browse </a>
            </li>

        </ul>
        </li>

    </ul>
</div>

<div data-role="view" id="view1">
    <div>
        Swipe from right to left to
          view the Drawer widget
    </div>
</div>

<div data-role="view" id="view2">
    <div>
        Browse view  in which Drawer is disabled.
    </div>
</div>


<script>
    var app = new kendo.mobile.Application(document.body, {
        skin: 'flat'
```

```
        });

        function onBeforeShow(e) {
            //check for view id to prevent
            //display of Drawer
            if (app.view().id == "#view2") {
                e.preventDefault();
            }
        }
    </script>
```

 Try it in jsFiddle:
http://jsfiddle.net/kendomobile/uEbgz/

We added two views with the IDs view1 and view2, in the example for the links Take Photo and Browse respectively. Then the beforeShow event of the Drawer widget is hooked to the event handler onBeforeShow, in which the current view's ID is checked using the method app.view().id. If the current view ID is #view2, we are calling the preventDefault() method of the Drawer so that it is not displayed in the second view.

Displaying a Drawer widget using navigational widgets

We saw in the previous sections that the Drawer widget can be displayed using swipes. Along with swipes, we can use any of the Kendo navigational widgets to open the Drawer widget. To facilitate this, we just need to point the href attribute of the navigational element to the ID of the Drawer that is prepended with a # and set data-rel="drawer" as shown in the following script:

```
<div data-role="drawer" id="my-drawer">

</div>

<div data-role="view">
    <a data-role="button"
        href="#my-drawer"
        data-rel="drawer">Open my drawer</a>
</div>
```

Now, let's see an example where we have both left and right Drawer widgets, with navigable menus and custom headers for the Drawers. Two buttons, **Open Left** and **Open Right**, are placed on the NavBar widget in the layout of the views, which can be clicked to open the Drawer widgets as shown in the following code:

```
<div data-role="layout" data-id="drawer-layout">
    <header data-role="header">
        <div data-role="navbar">
            <a data-role="button" data-rel="drawer"
                href="#left-drawer"  data-align="left">
                    Open Left
            </a>
            <span data-role="view-title"></span>
            <a data-role="button" data-rel="drawer"
                href="#right-drawer"  data-align="right">
                    Open Right
            </a>
        </div>
    </header>

</div>

<div data-role="drawer" id="left-drawer"
    data-views="['drawer-page1', 'drawer-page2', 'drawer-page3']">
    <ul data-role="listview" data-type="group">
        <li>Clickable Menu
            <ul>
                <li data-icon="favorites">
                    <a href="#drawer-page1">
                        Page 1
                    </a>
                </li>
                <li data-icon="downloads">
                    <a href="#drawer-page2"
                        >
                        Page 2</a>
                </li>
                <li data-icon="featured">
                    <a href="#drawer-page3">
                        Page 3</a>
                </li>
            </ul>
        </li>
```

```
        <li>Static Menu
            <ul>
                <li>Item 1</li>
                <li>Item 2</li>
                <li>Item 3</li>
            </ul>
        </li>
        </ul>
</div>

<div data-role="drawer" id="right-drawer"
    data-title="Two Way Menu"
    data-position="right" >
    <header data-role="header">
        <div data-role="navbar">
            <span data-role="view-title">
                Two Way Menu
            </span>
        </div>
    </header>
    <ul data-role="listview">
        <li >Right Item 1</li>
        <li >Right Item 2</li>
        <li >Right Item 3</li>
    </ul>
</div>

    <div data-role="view" id="drawer-page1"
        data-layout="drawer-layout"
        data-title="Page 1">
    <h1>Page 1 </h1>
</div>

<div data-role="view" id="drawer-page2"
    data-layout="drawer-layout"
    data-title="Page 2">
    <h1>Page 2 </h1>
</div>

    <div data-role="view" id="drawer-page3"
        data-layout="drawer-layout"
        data-title="Page 3">
        <h1>Page 3 </h1>
</div>

<script>
    var app = new kendo.mobile.Application(document.body);
</script>
```

Try it in jsFiddle:
`http://jsfiddle.net/kendomobile/sCb56/`

When the above app is loaded in **iOS 6**, it looks like the following screenshot, which has two buttons on either side of the app's navigation bar:

When one of the two buttons is clicked, the Drawer widget is opened from the respective side. The menu opened from left side has clickable links which will take you to different views. See the following screenshot:

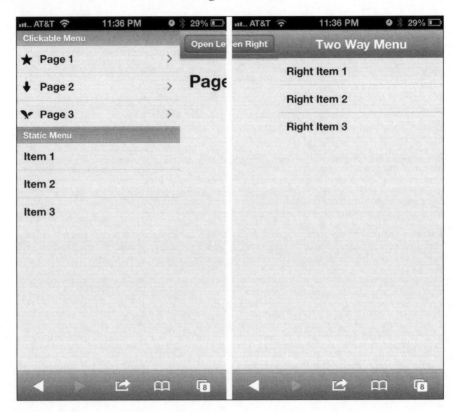

Summary

In this chapter, we explored more Kendo UI Mobile widgets, learned how to instantiate and use them in multiple scenarios hands-on, which helped us to create a solid foundation to complete our Movie Tickets application. In the next chapter, we will learn how to integrate most of these widgets using ASP.NET Web API services at the backend.

7
Movie Tickets Application – Complete Integration

In this chapter, we will complete our MovieTickets sample application, which we started in *Chapter 4*, *Integration Using Framework Elements*, by integrating with Kendo UI Mobile widgets, Framework elements, and the ASP.NET Web API service. We will implement views for a movie list, theater list, ticket purchase, and trailers. At the end of this chapter, you will be really amazed to see how easy it is to build a complete end-to-end mobile application with extensible, maintainable, and well-structured code using the Kendo UI Mobile Framework!

In this chapter we will cover:

- Completing the Web API service
- Frontend views
- Movie list screen
- Theater list screen
- Book Tickets screen
- Trailer videos slideshow screen

Completing the Web API service

In *Chapter 3, Service Layer with ASP.NET Web API*, we created a repository class called `MovieRepository.cs` with hardcoded data for a list of movies and theaters. We will use the same data here in this chapter to build the new views in our sample application.

> The full source code of both the Web API service and Kendo UI mobile is provided with the book at Packt Publishing's website. If you are not from a .NET background or not interested in creating the service layer, feel free to use the service hosted in this URL to connect to your frontend:
>
> `http://api.kendomobilebook.com/api/`
>
> For example, to get a list of **Now Playing** movies, the URL will be:
>
> `http://api.kendomobilebook.com/api/Movies/`
> `GetMovieList?listtype=0`
>
> The completed mobile application can be accessed online here:
>
> `http://movies.kendomobilebook.com`

Movie list

Open the `MovieTicketsBLL.cs` file and add the following `static` method to the `MovieTicketsBLL` class:

```
public static List<MovieBO> GetMovieList(int listType)
{
    var moviesMasterList = MovieRepository.GetMoviesMasterList();

    switch (listType)
    {
            //return now playing movies
        case 0:
            return moviesMasterList
                    .Where( m => m.IsNowPlaying == true )
                    .ToList();

        //return coming soon movies
        case 1:
            return moviesMasterList
                    .Where(m => m.IsNowPlaying == false)
                    .ToList();
```

```
        // return all the movies sorted by name
        default:
            return moviesMasterList
                    .OrderBy(x => x.Name)
                    .ToList();
    }
}
```

This method reads the list of movies from the repository, and returns the list depending on the type of the movie, which is defined by the input variable `listType`:

- `listType` = 0: Returns the **Now Playing** movies
- `listType` = 1: Returns the **Coming Soon** movies
- `listType` = 2: Returns all the movies sorted alphabetically in an ascending order

Now let's create an action method in `MoviesController.cs`, which calls the `GetMovieList` BLL method:

```
public List<MovieBO> GetMovieList(int listType)
{
    return MovieTicketsBLL.GetMovieList(listType);
}
```

Now we are all set with the service method, to list the movies in the initial view depending on the filter selected. To make sure that your service method is working, after building the service, hit this URL on your browser:

```
http://localhost/movietickets.webapi/api/Movies/
GetMovieList/?listType=0
```

You will get a response with all the now-playing movies listed, as shown in the following screenshot:

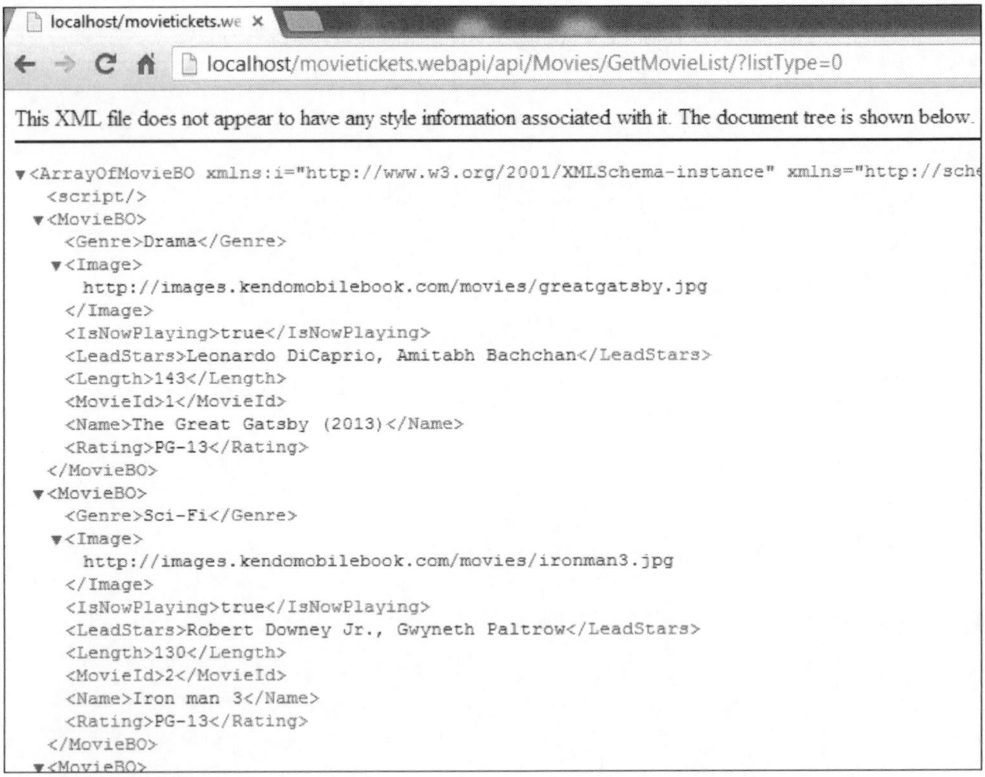

Movie trailers

This service method will return YouTube links of the movie trailers, which will be displayed in a ScrollView widget in the **Trailers** view of the application. Let's start by creating the business layer.

Create a class called `TrailerBO` inside the `BLL\BusinessObjects` directory:

```
public class TrailerBO
{
    public string MovieName { get; set; }
    public string VideoUrl { get; set; }
}
```

Repository

Now declare a class-level `static` variable in the `MovieRepository.cs` class:

```
public static List<TrailerBO> trailersMasterList;
```

We are creating a `static` list as the repository base data will be the same for all the requests, and so we need only one instance across the application. This variable will hold the list of trailers to be displayed in the application.

Now add the following methods in the `MovieRepository.cs` class:

```
//Method to create hardcode data for trailers
private static void CreateTrailersMasterList()
{
    trailersMasterList = new List<TrailerBO>()
    {
        new TrailerBO(){
            MovieName= "The Great Gatsby (2013)",
            VideoUrl= "http://www.youtube.com/embed/
rARN6agiW7o?html5=1"
        },
        new TrailerBO(){
            MovieName= "Iron Man 3",
            VideoUrl= "http://www.youtube.com/
embed/2CzoSeClcw0?html5=1"
        }
    }
}
```

This method creates a list of YouTube links for the movie trailers along with the movie names. You can add as many YouTube links as you need in this object; see this snippet from the source code:

```
//This method returns a list of
//trailer links and movie names
public static List<TrailerBO> GetTrailersMasterList()
{
    if (trailersMasterList == null
        || trailersMasterList.Count == 0)
    {
        CreateTrailersMasterList();
    }
    return trailersMasterList;
}
```

This method loads the `trailersMasterList` object with data if it's not already loaded, and returns it. The business layer calls this method to retrieve the list of trailers.

Business layer

In the BLL file `MovieTicketsBLL.cs`, add the following method, which returns the list of trailers to the controller action method:

```
public static List<TrailerBO> GetTrailers()
{
    return MovieRepository.GetTrailersMasterList();
}
```

Action method

Now in `MoviesController.cs`, add the following action method which returns the list of trailers:

```
public List<TrailerBO> GetTrailers()
{
    return MovieTicketsBLL.GetTrailers();
}
```

Action method for ticketing

We need one more controller and an action method which will be called for purchasing tickets. This is a POST method that takes a ticket object as an input. Since we don't have a database, we won't do any further processing in this controller method and just return a true value to flag that the ticketing was successful.

Now create a file called `TicketPurchaseBO.cs` inside the `BLL\BusinessObjects` directory with the following code:

```
public class TicketPurchaseBO
{
    public string TheaterId { get; set; }
    public string MovieId { get; set; }
    public int NoOfChildTickets { get; set; }
    public int NoOfAdultTickets { get; set; }
    public string ShowDate { get; set; }
    public string ShowTime { get; set; }
    public string TotalAmount { get; set; }
}
```

Now create a controller called `TicketController` and add a POST action to it:

```
// POST api/tickets
public bool Post(TicketPurchaseBO ticket)
{
    //implement save logic here. For the sake of simplicity
    //we assume that the ticket is saved properly and
    //return a success boolean.

    return true;
}
```

We will use this action method in the final screen of the ticketing workflow from the movie list view.

This completes the setup of our Web API service methods, and allows us to build the screens of our Movie Tickets application.

Frontend views

Now let's start building the pending two sections of our frontend:

- Movie listing and ticketing workflow:
    ◦ **Movies** list with filter
    ◦ **Theaters** list of selected movie
    ◦ **Book Tickets** screen

- Movie trailers

Configuration

Let's create the Web API URLs in our `configuration.js` file so that we don't have to use hardcoded strings inside the application:

```
MovieTickets.configuration = (function () {
var serviceUrl = "http://localhost/movietickets.webapi/api/";

    return {
        serviceUrl: serviceUrl,
        accountUrl: serviceUrl + "Account/",
        getMovieListUrl: serviceUrl + "Movies/GetMovieList/",
        getTheaterListForMovieUrl: serviceUrl +
            "Theater/Get/",
```

```
                    getTrailersUrl: serviceUrl + "Movies/GetTrailers/",
                    purchaseTicketsUrl: serviceUrl + "Tickets"
        }
    })();
```

If you want to use the hosted service provided by us, you can replace the declaration of `serviceUrl` with the application of the following code snippet:

```
var serviceUrl = "http://api.kendomobilebook.com/
api/"
```

The Movie list screen

This is the initial view of the application where a list of movies is displayed. In a real-world application, the list may be all the movies playing close to the user's location. This list can be found using the HTML5 Geolocation API, or by using this profile information. For the sake of simplicity, we are just displaying a list of movies using a search-enabled `ListView` widget. The screen will have a `ButtonGroup` widget at the top with three filter options shown as:

- **Now Playing**
- **Coming Soon**
- **A-Z**

Depending on the filter selection, movies will be loaded in the list. Once you tap on a movie list item, a list of theaters is shown in the next screen. Users can choose a theater and then tap on the movie timing to proceed to the next, **Book Tickets**, screen. This is the last screen where tickets can be purchased and the transaction is completed.

The workflow of the application starting from the initial screen is shown as follows:

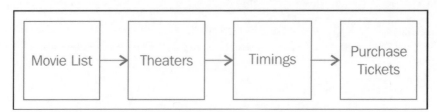

Once we complete this view and wire it with the data from the service, our app will look like the following screenshots:

The JavaScript module

Let's create the JavaScript module `movieList` for the **Movies** list view by defining the ViewModel of the view and other methods within the namespace `MovieTickets`.

We will add methods to fetch data from the service to load the `viewModel` object, and initialize the view and event handler when the type of movie list is changed from the UI. The movie list filter is implemented using a `ButtonGroup` widget with these options: **Now Playing**, **Coming Soon**, and **A-Z**:

```
MovieTickets.movieList = (function(){

    var viewModel = kendo.observable({
        movieList: {}
    });
});
```

```javascript
    //fetches the list of movies from the service
    //depending on the listType filter
    function getMovieList(listType) {
        var movieListoptions = {
            url: MovieTickets.configuration.getMovieListUrl,
            data: { listType: listType },
            requestType: "GET",
            dataType: "JSON",
            callBack: callBack
        };
        //service call
        MovieTickets.dataAccess.callService(movieListoptions);
    }
    //callback method from service call
    function callBack(result) {
        if (result.success === true) {
            viewModel.set("movieList", result.data);
        }
    }


    //this event is fired when movie list
    //type is changed from the UI
    function listTypeSelected(e) {

        getMovieList(e.sender.selectedIndex);
    }
    //Loading the movie list with listType= 0
    //which is Now Running list
    function init(){
        getMovieList(0);
    }

    return {
        initialize: init,
        getMovieList: getMovieList,
        viewModel: viewModel,
        listTypeSelected:listTypeSelected
    }

})();
```

Let's check out some important sections of this code:

- `getMovieList`: This method calls the Web API service using the `MovieTickets.dataAccess` module and updates the `viewModel` object with the returned data from the `callBack` method. The `GetMovieList` action method of the `MoviesController` is invoked to retrieve the movie list.

- `listTypeSelected`: This is the event fired at the time of changing the movie list type filter (`Now Playing`, `Coming Soon`, and `A-Z`). In this event handler, the `getMovieList` method is called using the selected filter as input.

- `init`: This method calls the `getMovieList()` method with the first filter item **Now Playing** as input. This is the default filter.

In the return statement, all the `public` objects and methods are returned so that they can be accessed by prefixing `MovieTickets.movieList` to their names.

The Movie list view

In *Chapter 2, Building Your First Mobile Application*, we defined the view for the **Movies** list screen in the `index.html` file. Let's pick the code from where we left off in *Chapter 2* and start building the UI components. The movie list will be displayed using a Kendo `ListView` widget. Each list item contains the following:

- Image of the movie
- Movie name
- Genre
- Rating
- Length of the movie
- Lead actors

When we tap on any one of the movie items from the **Now Playing** list, the view should navigate to the Theaters list view with the ID `mt-theaters-movie-view`.

The List item template

The previous data needs to be rendered in the ListView widget, and for that, we need to create a Kendo UI template as shown in the following code:

```
<!--template for movie list -->
<script type="text/x-kendo-template" id="mt-main-tmpl-movie-list">
    # var ecodedURI = '\\#mt-theaters-movie-view?movieId=' +
                        MovieId + '&movieName=' +
                        encodeURIComponent(Name) + '&rating=' +
                        Rating + '&image=' + Image #

    #if(IsNowPlaying !== true){
        ecodedURI= "";
        }#

<a href="#:ecodedURI#" >
    <img class="mt-movie-photo" src="#:Image#" />
    <div class="mt-movie-details">
      <span class="mt-listitem-title"> #:Name# </span>
      <span data-bind="invisible:IsNowPlaying"
            class="mt-highlight-label2">[Coming Soon]</span><br/>
      <span class="mt-normal-label"> #:Genre#, </span>
      <span class="mt-normal-label"> #:Length# Mins </span>
      <span class="mt-highlight-label"> #:Rating# </span> <br/>
      <span class="mt-normal-label"> #:LeadStars# </span>
    </div>
    </a>
</script>
```

This template creates placeholders for all the attributes of a movie and wraps it around an anchor tag and sets the `href` attribute to navigate to the **Theater** list view (ID `mt-theaters-movie-view`) with all the properties of the selected movie as query strings.

Encoding URI

The URI for redirection is created using a variable `encodedURI` inside the template. Once the URI is properly formed, the value of this variable is set as the anchor tag's `href` value. The JavaScript method `encodeURIComponent` is used to make movie names safe to transfer via URIs, as movie names may contain special characters which may mess up URIs.

Unreleased movies should not have navigation enabled, as there won't be a list of theaters to be displayed and tickets cannot be booked. So if the property IsNowPlaying is not true, we are setting the value of ecodedURI as an empty string so that at the time of tapping on a **Coming Soon** movie, navigation does not occur.

We are designing a movie list item template so that the selected movie's details are transferred to the redirected view using query strings rather than sharing JavaScript objects within the application. One advantage of implementing this method is that, during development, once we make changes to the redirected view, we can see/debug the changes just by refreshing the browser as all the data to load the view is available in the URL, unlike JavaScript objects which loses data when the browser is refreshed.

Styles

The following styles are also added to the Styles.css file to style the contents of the template:

```css
.mt-movie-photo {
    float:left;
    height:90px;
    width:70px;
}

.mt-listitem-title {
    font-size:19px;
    font-weight:bold;
    color:darkblue;

}

.mt-highlight-label {
    color:maroon;
}

.mt-highlight-label2 {
    color:green;
}
```

Configuring view and ListView

In the view definition we can now add the ListView widget, wire up the `init` event, and set the `model` property as shown in the following code:

```
<!-- Movies main view --->
<div data-role="view" id="mt-home-main-view" data-title="Movies"
        data-init="MovieTickets.movieList.initialize"
        data-model="MovieTickets.movieList.viewModel"
        data-layout="mt-main-layout" class="no-backbutton">

    <!--Movie List -->
    <ul id="mt-main-movie-list-view" data-role="listview"
        data-template="mt-main-tmpl-movie-list"
        data-filterable="{field:'Name', operator:'startsWith'}"
        data-bind="source:movieList">
    </ul>

</div>
```

In the ListView widget, we set the template ID, made the widget filterable using the first name, and bound the data source as `movieList` which is a property of `MovieTickets.movieList.viewModel`. Since we are setting the `model` property of the view as the `MovieTickets.movieList.viewModel` object, all the properties of this object are available inside the view and we can use them without prefixing them with the parent object's names. At the time of navigating to the application, we can see the list of **Now Playing** movies.

Movie list type ButtonGroup

As mentioned earlier, in our application we have three types of movie lists: Now
Playing, Coming Soon and A-Z. A **ButtonGroup** is the most suitable Kendo UI
widget in this scenario to filter movies using the three list types. Let's now add a
ButtonGroup widget above the ListView widget to select the type of list by adding
the following code:

```
<ul data-role="buttongroup" data-index="0"
    data-select="MovieTickets.movieList.listTypeSelected">
    <li>Now Playing</li>
    <li>Coming Soon</li>
    <li>A-Z</li>
</ul>
```

The select event is bound to the MovieTickets.movieList.listTypeSelected
event, which is defined in the movieList module. To change the default iOS-specific
colors of the ButtonGroup widget, we can add the following styles in Styles.css:

```
.km-ios #mt-home-main-view .km-buttongroup .km-button:not(.km-
state-active) {
    width:70px;
    font-size: 1em;
    background-color:gray;
    color:white;
    text-shadow:none;
}
.km-ios #mt-home-main-view .km-buttongroup .km-state-active {
    width:70px;
    font-size: 1em;
    background-color:#FF6600;
    color:white;
    background-image:none;
}
```

The previous styles make the ButtonGroup widget's default background color gray and the selected button's background color orange.

Tapping on the ButtonGroup widget's buttons will now load the ListView widget with the movie type selected.

Theaters list screen

Once the user selects a movie by tapping on the item in the **Movie** list screen, the user is redirected to the **Theater** list screen where a list of theaters with addresses and showtimings is displayed.

The JavaScript module

Let's start building this screen by creating the JavaScript module with ViewModel for the view and associated methods. Create a file called theaters-movie-list.js in the js folder and add its reference in the index.html file. The design of the module is similar to that of the **Movies** list screen:

```
MovieTickets.theaterListForMovie = (function () {

    //ViewModel to be bound to the view
    var viewModel = kendo.observable({
        theaterList: {},
        selectedMovie: {
```

```
            movieId: "",
            movieName: "",
            rating: "",
            imageUrl:""
        },
        selectedDate: ""

    });


    //retrieve list of theaters from the service
    function getTheaterList(movieId) {
        var serviceOptions =
            {
            url: MovieTickets.configuration
.getTheaterListForMovieUrl,
            data: { movieId: movieId },
            requestType: "GET",
            dataType: "JSON",
            callBack: callBack
        };
        MovieTickets.dataAccess.callService(serviceOptions);


    }

    function callBack(result) {
        if (result.success === true) {
            viewModel.set("theaterList", result.data);
        }
    }

    //handler for show event of the view
    function show(e) {

    //hard coding today's date for selected date
        viewModel.set('selectedDate', new
Date().toLocaleDateString());

        //read the selected movie's details from the query string
        viewModel.set("selectedMovie", {
            movieId: e.view.params.movieId,
         movieName:
         decodeURIComponent(e.view.params.movieName),
            rating: e.view.params.rating,
            imageUrl: e.view.params.image
```

```
        });
        getTheaterList(e.view.params.movieId);
    }

    return {
        show: show,
        getTheaterList: getTheaterList,
        viewModel: viewModel,
    }
})();
```

Let's take a look at the properties and methods of the `viewModel` object:

- `theaterList`: It contains the list of theaters with addresses and showtimings.

- `selectedMovie`: This object holds the details of the movie selected from the movie list view. This object is initialized in the show event of the view and property values are read from the query string.

- `selectedDate`: This object contains the date for which the showtimings are shown. In our sample application, it's always the current date.

- `getTheaterList(movieId)`: This method fetches the list of theaters from the service and the result is loaded into the `theaterList` property of the `viewModel` object. We are using the `Get` action method of the `Theater` controller.

- `show(e)`: This is the event handler method for the `show` event of the view. Query string values available in the collection `e.view.params` are extracted and assigned to the properties of the `selectedMovie` object. The `getTheaterList()` method is called as the last step in this event handler.

Theaters list view

Let's now open up `index.html` and configure the **Theaters** list view. The model property of the view is set as `MovieTickets.theaterListForMovie.viewModel` and the show event is wired to `MovieTickets.theaterListForMovie.show`.

All the properties of the selected movies are bound to HTML elements using the `data-bind` attribute of Kendo MVVM:

```
<div data-role="view" id="mt-theaters-movie-view"
    data-model="MovieTickets.theaterListForMovie.viewModel"
    data-show="MovieTickets.theaterListForMovie.show"
    data-layout="mt-main-layout" data-title="Theaters">
    <div id="mt-theaters-movie-details">
```

```
    <img class="mt-movie-photo"
        data-bind="attr: { src: selectedMovie.imageUrl}" />
    <div class="mt-movie-details">
        <div class="mt-listitem-title"
            data-bind="text: selectedMovie.movieName"></div>

        <div class="mt-highlight-label"
            data-bind="text: selectedMovie.rating"></div>

    Date: <span class="mt-highlight-label"
                data-bind="text: selectedDate"></span>
    </div>
</div>
<hr />

<!-- Theater ListView goes here -->

</div>
```

Theaters list template

In the **Theaters** list view, we will also use a `ListView` widget and render the list items using a Kendo template.

Create a template as shown in the following code:

```
<script type="text/x-kendo-template"
  id="mt-main-tmpl-theater-list">
        <!-- redirect URI-->
          #var ecodedURI = 'theaterName=' +
encodeURIComponent( Name ) +
                '&address=' + encodeURIComponent( Address ) +
                '&movieName=' + encodeURIComponent(
MovieTickets.theaterListForMovie.viewModel.selectedMovie.movieName) +
                '&rating=' + MovieTickets.theaterListForMovie.
viewModel.selectedMovie.rating +
                '&movieId=' + MovieTickets.theaterListForMovie.
viewModel.selectedMovie.movieId +
                '&theaterId=' + TheaterId +
                '&date=' + encodeURIComponent(
MovieTickets.theaterListForMovie.viewModel.selectedDate )
        #

        <div>
            <span class="mt-title"> #:Name# </span>
```

```
            <span class="mt-highlight-label"> #:MilesFromCurrentLoc#
Miles </span><br/>
            <span class="mt-normal-label"> #:Address# </span>

        <div>
            <!--  render show times -->
            #for(var i=0; i < Timings.length; i++) {#
            <a class="mt-timings"
                href="\\#BookTickets.html?#:ecodedURI#
                &time=#:encodeURIComponent(Timings[i])#">
                #:Timings[i]#</a>

            <!--Add pipe separator for show times -->
            #if(i < (Timings.length - 1)){#
                |
<!--The pipe separator won't appear for the last item -->
            #}#
            #}#
        </div>
    </div>

</script>
```

The theater and showtime of the movie is selected by the user by tapping on the rendered show times. After a showtime is selected, the user is redirected to the **Book Tickets** view with details about the selected movie, theaters and showtimes in the query string. For this purpose, we are creating the URI using the variable encodedURI in the template as done in the **Movie** list view. The details of the theaters such as the theater name, address, and showtimes are rendered using the template with the showtimes list separated using a pipe (|) symbol.

The CSS class mt-timings is added to Styles.css to style the showtimes appearing on the screen:

```
.mt-timings{
    color:green !important;
    text-decoration: none !important;
}
```

Adding ListView for theaters

The last step in the **Theaters** list view is to add a Kendo ListView widget and render it using the template we created in the previous section.

Add the following Kendo ListView widget as the final item in the view definition with the `theaterList` property of the ViewModel object, which is bound to the list view as its data source:

```
<ul id="mt-theaters-movie-list" data-role="listview"
        data-template="mt-main-tmpl-theater-list"
        data-bind="source:theaterList">
</ul>
```

Now we are all set to run our app, select a movie from the initial screen, and view the **Theaters** list screen!

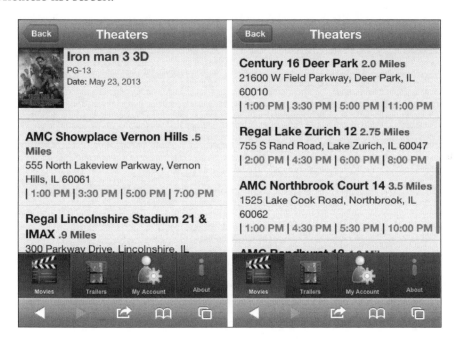

Book Tickets screen

The final screen in our Movie Tickets app's ticketing workflow is the **Book Tickets** screen, where users can select and purchase tickets for both adults and children. Both ticket types will have add and subtract buttons, in the form of icons with a plus (**+**) and minus (**-**) symbol, bound by Kendo MVVM bindings, which will add and subtract the number of tickets for each type, display the total amount for each section as well as update the grand total.

Purchase is completed by clicking on the **Purchase** button which will send the ticket details to the service.

JavaScript module

Let's create a file called book-tickets.js in the js folder and add a JS module named MovieTickets.bookTickets, as shown in the following code, in the file:

```
MovieTickets.bookTickets = (function () {

    var viewModel = kendo.observable({

        //method to increment no of child tickets
        incrementChildTicket: function () {

            this.set("noChildTickets", parseInt(
                        this.get("noChildTickets")) + 1);
        },

        //method to increment no of adult tickets
        incrementAdultTicket: function () {

            this.set("noAdultTickets", parseInt(
                        this.get("noAdultTickets")) + 1);
        },

        //method to decrement no of child tickets
        decrementChildTicket: function () {
            if (this.get("noChildTickets") !=0 )
                this.set("noChildTickets", parseInt(
                            this.get("noChildTickets")) - 1);
        },

        //method to decrement no of adult tickets
        decrementAdultTicket: function () {
```

```
            if (this.get("noAdultTickets") != 0)
                this.set("noAdultTickets", parseInt(
                        this.get("noAdultTickets")) - 1);
        },

        //get the total amount for adult ickets
        noAdultTotalAmount: function () {
                return this.get("noAdultTickets") * 10.00
        },

        //get the total amount for child tickets
        noChildTotalAmount: function () {
                return this.get("noChildTickets") * 8.00
        },

        //get total amount
        totalAmount: function () {
            return viewModel.noAdultTotalAmount() +
                    viewModel.noChildTotalAmount();
        },

        noAdultTickets: 0,
        noChildTickets: 0,

        //movie details
        selectedMovie: {
            movieId: "",
            movieName: "",
            rating: "",
        },
        //teater details
        selectedTheater: {
            theaterId: "",
            theaterName: "",
            address: "",
            time:""
        },
    });

})();
```

The `viewModel` object has the following functions:

- `incrementChildTicket()`
- `incrementAdultTicket()`
- `decrementChildTicket()`
- `decrementAdultTicket()`
- `noChildTotalAmount()`
- `noAdultTotalAmount()`
- `totalAmount()`

Functionalities of these methods are self-explanatory. The properties `noAdultTickets` and `noChildTickets` will hold the total number of adult and child tickets respectively. The `selectedMovie` and `selectedTheater` properties will be loaded with the movie and theater for which the booking is made.

Show event

In the `show` event, properties of the `viewModel` object `selectedMovie` and `selectedTheater` is loaded by reading respective values from the query string. Now add this `show` event in our `MovieTickets.bookTickets` module right after the `viewModel` definition:

```
function show(e) {
    viewModel.set("selectedMovie", {
        movieId: e.view.params.movieId,
        movieName: decodeURIComponent(e.view.params.movieName),
        rating: e.view.params.rating,
    });
    viewModel.set("selectedTheater", {
        theaterId: e.view.params.theaterId,
        theaterName: decodeURIComponent(e.view.params.theaterName),
        address: decodeURIComponent(e.view.params.address),
        time: decodeURIComponent(e.view.params.time),
        date: decodeURIComponent(e.view.params.date)
    });
}
```

Purchase tickets

Now let's add a function called `purchaseTickets()` to the `MovieTickets.`
`bookTickets` module. In this method, we will check whether at least one ticket
is selected by the user, otherwise an alert message is displayed to the user. Once the
ticket is validated, all the data that is required for booking tickets is sent as an HTTP
POST to the `Tickets` controller in our Web API service. Once the ticket purchase
is successful, a success message is displayed to the user in a Kendo Mobile
ModalView widget:

```
//method to purchase tickets. This method sends
//all the data to the service in an HTTP POST
function purchaseTickets() {

    //no tickets are selected, display a message
    if (viewModel.noAdultTickets == 0 &&
        viewModel.noChildTickets == 0) {
        alert('Atleast one ticket needs to be purchased.');
        return;
    }

    var serviceOptions = {
        url: MovieTickets.configuration.purchaseTicketsUrl,
        data: {
            movieId: viewModel.selectedMovie.movieId,
            theaterId: viewModel.selectedTheater.theaterId,
            noOfAdultTickets: viewModel.noAdultTickets,
            noOfChildTickets: viewModel.noChildTickets,
            showDate: viewModel.selectedTheater.date,
            showTime: viewModel.selectedTheater.time,
            totalAmount: viewModel.totalAmount
        },
        requestType: "POST",
        dataType: "JSON",
        callBack: purchaseCallBack
    }
    //service call.
    MovieTickets.dataAccess.callService(serviceOptions);

    function purchaseCallBack(result) {
        if (result.success === true) {
            //display a message to the user
            //using modal view
```

```
            var intializedModalView =
                $("#mt-modal-complete").data("kendoMobileModalView");

            //if the modal view is already initialized,
            //destroy it
            if (intializedModalView) {
                intializedModalView.destroy();
            }

            $('#mt-modal-complete').kendoMobileModalView({
                height: 130, width: 200
            }).data("kendoMobileModalView").open();

        } else {
            alert('purchase failed. please try again.');
        }
    }
}
```

The last method that we need to add to this module is the method to close
the ModalView widget and redirect to the home page after the ticket booking
is successful:

```
//method to close the modal view and redirect
//to the main view.
function closeModalView() {

    //close the confirmation modal popup
    $("#mt-modal-complete").data("kendoMobileModalView").close();

    //navigate to the home page
    MovieTickets.main.getKendoApplication().navigate('#mt-home-main-
view');
}
```

The Book Tickets view

For the Book Tickets view, let's create an external HTML file called `BookTickets.html` in the root folder and add a Kendo Mobile view as shown in the following code snippet:

```
<div data-role="view"
    data-title="Book Tickets" data-layout="mt-main-layout"
    data-show="MovieTickets.bookTickets.show"
    data-model="MovieTickets.bookTickets.viewModel"
    id="mt-book-tickets-view">
</div>
```

The title of the view is set as **Book Tickets**, the show event of the view is wired to the `MovieTickets.bookTickets.show` method and `MovieTickets.bookTickets.viewModel` is set as the model of the view. In this view, we will add two sections, The first one is the movie details section, where we display the movie name, rating, theater name, address, date, and time. In the second section, we provide the buttons for adding and removing tickets with textboxes so that the users can select the number of tickets for adults and children. At the bottom of the screen, a button to complete the purchase is added. To display the movie details section, we will use a ListView widget with two list items. The data will be displayed in `<span>` elements using **MVVM** `data-bind` attributes:

```
<ul data-role="listview">
    <li>
        <span class="mt-listitem-title"
                data-bind="text: selectedMovie.movieName">
        </span>
        <span class="mt-highlight-label"
                data-bind="text: selectedMovie.rating">
        </span>
        <br />
    </li>
    <li>
        <span class="mt-title"
                data-bind="text: selectedTheater.theaterName">
        </span>
        <br />
        <span class="mt-normal-label"
                data-bind="text: selectedTheater.address">
        </span>
        <br />
```

```
        <span class="mt-normal-label">Date:</span>
        <span class="mt-highlight-label"
                data-bind="text: selectedTheater.date">
        </span>
        <span class="mt-highlight-label"
                data-bind="text: selectedTheater.time"></span>
    </li>
</ul>
```

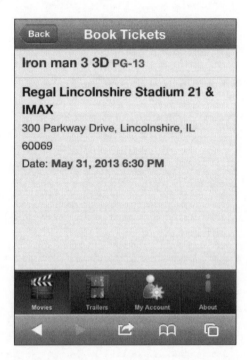

In the second section, we will add the contents in a ListView widget. We will display the total amount for adults and children, as well as the grand total on the screen and update the numbers automatically when a ticket count is updated by the user. This is achieved by binding the UI elements to the properties and methods of our Observable `viewModel`, which is already done in the view definition by setting:

```
data-model= "MovieTickets.bookTickets.viewModel"
```

Now let's add the HTML for the second section:

```
<ul data-role="listview" data-style="inset">
    <li>
        <div>
            Adult:
            <br />
```

```
            <img src="images/add.png" class="mt-list-image"
                    data-bind="click:incrementAdultTicket" />
            <input type="text" data-bind="value:noAdultTickets"
                    class="mt-ticket-num-input" />

            <img src="images/remove.png" class="mt-list-image"
                data-bind="click:decrementAdultTicket" />
            x 10.00 = $
            <label data-bind="text:noAdultTotalAmount"></label>
        </div>
    </li>
    <li>
        <div>
            Child:
            <br />
            <img src="images/add.png" class="mt-list-image"
                    data-bind="click:incrementChildTicket" />
            <input type="text" data-bind="value:noChildTickets"
                    class="mt-ticket-num-input" />
            <img src="images/remove.png" class="mt-list-image"
                    data-bind="click:decrementChildTicket" />
            x 8.00 =
        $<label data-bind="text:noChildTotalAmount"></label>
        </div>
    </li>
    <li>
        <div>
            <span class="mt-title">Total: </span>
            <span class="mt-total-amount">
                $<label data-bind="text:totalAmount"></label>
            </span>
        </div>
    </li>
    <li>
        <div>
          <a data-role="button" class="mt-purchase-button"
            data-click="MovieTickets.bookTickets.purchaseTickets">
                Purchase
          </a>
        </div>
    </li>
</ul>
```

Add the following CSS to `Style.css` to beautify the UI:

```
.mt-ticket-num-input {
    width: 45px !important;
    position: relative !important;
    border: ridge !important;
    min-width: 45px !important;
}
.mt-total-amount {
    color:orangered;
    font-size:25px;
}
.mt-list-image {
    vertical-align:middle;
}

.mt-purchase-button {
    background-color: orangered !important;
    width:100px;
}
```

If we click on the **Purchase** button, the ticket details are sent to the server and if the callback result is successful, a message is displayed to the user.

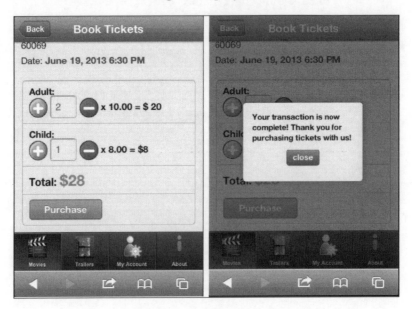

Creating the trailer videos slideshow screen

Let's now create the final screen of our application, which displays a slideshow of the movie trailers, which are videos hosted on YouTube. We are using the Kendo UI Mobile ScrollView widget for this purpose.

In this view, video links and movie names are received from the service and the video links are added to an <iframe> element defined in a Kendo UI template.

HTML

Let's open up the Trailers.html file, which we created in *Chapter 2, Building Your First Mobile Application*, and add the following HTML:

```
<div data-role="view" data-title="Trailers"
    data-show="MovieTickets.trailers.show"
    data-layout="mt-main-layout" id="mt-trailers-view">
  <div id="mt-trailer-scrollview" data-role="scrollview">

  </div>
  <!-- In order for the pages to be rendered properly
       make sure that you don't leave empty spaces
       between template's script tags and the html contents.
  -->
  <script type="text/x-kendo-template"
          id="mt-tmpl-trailers"><div data-role="page"
              class="mt-trailer-item">
      <div class="mt-listitem-title">#:MovieName# </div>
      <div>
       <iframe width="220" src="#:VideoUrl#"></iframe>
      </div>
      </div>
  </script>
</div>
```

In the previous HTML, we defined a ScrollView widget and the template with the ID mt-tmpl-trailers for contents to be loaded in the ScrollView. A Kendo template is also defined with the ID mt-tmpl-trailers in which the movie name is displayed on top and the video URL is embedded in an <iframe> element so that the video thumbnail is displayed on the view. Now we just need the data from the service to feed the template, and assign the rendered HTML inside the ScrollView widget.

The JavaScript module

Create a file called `trailers.js` in the `js` folder and add the following module code in the file:

```
MovieTickets.trailers = (function () {

    function show(e) {
        var options = {
            url: MovieTickets.configuration.getTrailersUrl,
            requestType: "GET",
            dataType: "JSON",
            callBack: callBack
        };
        MovieTickets.dataAccess.callService(options);
    }

    function callBack(result) {
      if (result.success === true) {

        var trailerTemplate = kendo.template(
$("#mt-trailers-view #mt-tmpl-trailers").html());

        $("#mt-trailers-view #mt-trailer-scrollview")
                .data('kendoMobileScrollView')
                .content(kendo.render(trailerTemplate,
    result.data));
        }
    }

    return {
        show: show
    }

})();
```

Now add this CSS class to `Style.css` to center align the videos:

```
.mt-trailer-item {
    text-align:center;
}
```

In the show event of the view, an Ajax call is fired to retrieve the list of videos to be displayed on the slide show. Once the data is received, it is provided as a content to the template defined in the view and the trailer slideshow is generated on the fly.

To accomplish this, in our code we first read the contents of the template into a variable with the name `trailerTemplate`. Then the template is rendered to HTML using the `kendo.render()` method, using the data returned by the service, and is fed as the content of the ScrollView widget as shown:

```
$("#mt-trailers-view #mt-trailer-scrollview")
                .data('kendoMobileScrollView')
                .content(kendo.render(trailerTemplate,
    result.data));
```

If we navigate to the **Trailers** view by clicking on the **Trailers** tab item, we can see the videos being displayed. Swiping to the left or right will display the movie trailers one by one.

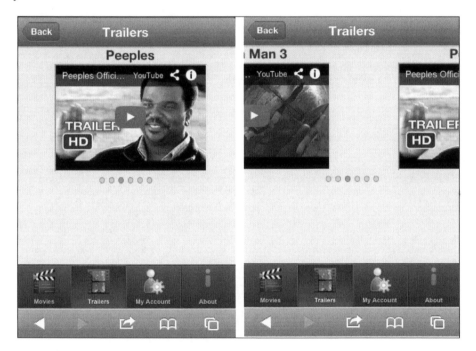

 You can visit `http://movies.kendomobilebook.com` to view the complete application.

Summary

In this chapter, we completed our Movie Tickets sample application by building functionalities that work with live data by connecting to an HTTP-based service built using ASP.NET Web API. We learned how to use important Kendo UI Mobile widgets and framework elements in a real-life application and saw how easy it is to build a mobile app using the Kendo UI Mobile Framework. You are now ready to build highly performing HTML5-based mobile applications using the Kendo UI Mobile Framework! Happy coding!

Index

B

C

D

E

F

 **Thank you for buying**
Building Mobile Applications Using Kendo UI Mobile and ASP.NET Web API

About Packt Publishing

Packt, pronounced 'packed', published its first book "*Mastering phpMyAdmin for Effective MySQL Management*" in April 2004 and subsequently continued to specialize in publishing highly focused books on specific technologies and solutions.

Our books and publications share the experiences of your fellow IT professionals in adapting and customizing today's systems, applications, and frameworks. Our solution based books give you the knowledge and power to customize the software and technologies you're using to get the job done. Packt books are more specific and less general than the IT books you have seen in the past. Our unique business model allows us to bring you more focused information, giving you more of what you need to know, and less of what you don't.

Packt is a modern, yet unique publishing company, which focuses on producing quality, cutting-edge books for communities of developers, administrators, and newbies alike. For more information, please visit our website: www.packtpub.com.

Writing for Packt

We welcome all inquiries from people who are interested in authoring. Book proposals should be sent to author@packtpub.com. If your book idea is still at an early stage and you would like to discuss it first before writing a formal book proposal, contact us; one of our commissioning editors will get in touch with you.

We're not just looking for published authors; if you have strong technical skills but no writing experience, our experienced editors can help you develop a writing career, or simply get some additional reward for your expertise.

Learning Kendo UI Web Development

ISBN: 978-1-849694-34-6   Paperback: 288 pages

An easy-to-follow practical tutorial to add exciting features to your web pages without being a JavaScript expert

1. Learn from clear and specific examples on how to utilize the full range of the Kendo UI tool set for the web

2. Add powerful tools to your website supported by a familiar and trusted name in innovative technology

3. Learn how to add amazing features with clear examples and make your website more interactive without being a JavaScript expert

Sencha Touch Mobile JavaScript Framework

ISBN: 978-1-849515-10-8   Paperback: 316 pages

Build web applications for Apple iOS and Google Android touchscreen devices with this first HTML5 mobile framework

1. Learn to develop web applications that look and feel native on Apple iOS and Google Android touchscreen devices using Sencha Touch through examples

2. Design resolution-independent and graphical representations like buttons, icons, and tabs of unparalleled flexibility

3. Add custom events like tap, double tap, swipe, tap and hold, pinch, and rotate

Please check **www.PacktPub.com** for information on our titles

Creating Mobile Apps with Sencha Touch 2

ISBN: 978-1-849518-90-1   Paperback: 348 pages

Learn to use the Sencha Touch programming language and expand your skills by building 10 unique applications

1. Learn the Sencha Touch programming language by building real, working applications

2. Each chapter focuses on different features and programming approaches; you can decide which is right for you

3. Full of well-explained example code and rich with screenshots

PhoneGap 2.x Mobile Application Development Hotshot

ISBN: 978-1-849519-40-3   Paperback: 388 pages

Create exciting apps for mobile devices using PhoneGap

1. Ten apps included to help you get started on your very own exciting mobile app

2. These apps include working with localization, social networks, geolocation, as well as the camera, audio, video, plugins, and more

3. Apps cover the spectrum from productivity apps, educational apps, all the way to entertainment and games

Please check **www.PacktPub.com** for information on our titles

Printed in Great Britain
by Amazon.co.uk, Ltd.,
Marston Gate.